A TIFFANY MONDAY
An Unusual Love Story

JOHN SAGER

WESTBOW
PRESS
A DIVISION OF THOMAS NELSON

WestBow Press books may be ordered through booksellers or by contacting:

WestBow Press
A Division of Thomas Nelson
1663 Liberty Drive
Bloomington, IN 47403
www.westbowpress.com
1-(866) 928-1240

Because of the dynamic nature of the Internet, any web addresses or links contained in this book may have changed since publication and may no longer be valid. The views expressed in this work are solely those of the author and do not necessarily reflect the views of the publisher, and the publisher hereby disclaims any responsibility for them.

Certain stock imagery © Thinkstock.
Any people depicted in stock imagery provided by Thinkstock are models, and such images are being used for illustrative purposes only.

ISBN: 978-1-4497-3213-4 (sc)
ISBN: 978-1-4497-3214-1 (hc)
ISBN: 978-1-4497-3212-7 (e)

Library of Congress Control Number: 2011961004

Printed in the United States of America

WestBow Press rev. date: 1/24/2012

DEDICATION

To my beloved Joan, easily the most beautiful person I have ever known. Her love for God, for life and for so many others has made their world much better.

Вечная Любовь = Eternal Love
John taught Joan to speak these two words in Russian. An intimate and beautiful toast, usually with a straight-up martini before dinner, clinking glasses and smiling deeply into each other's eyes.

PROLOGUE

This is a true story, nearly all of it taken verbatim from e-mail messages exchanged between two septuagenarians during the Winter, Spring and Summer of 2005. The names are real although some specific situations have been fictionalized. John has penned these words as an encouragement to other seniors because, although his and Joan's circumstances were unusual, the principle is the same: Keep the flames of love alive and never give in to the notion that it is too late.

Their married life became a culmination of a love that began, for John, in the Fall of 1935, when he entered Sumner Grade School in Washington State. Joan, pronounced Jo-ANN, who was also a first-grader, would become his wife some seventy years later.

John fell in love with Joan on the playgrounds of that school. Most guys get over this kind of early-on puppy love, John never did. He sensed, even at a young age, that Joan was something very special, far beyond "cute," and he admired her (even worshipped her, as he would later confess) for all that she was then, as a child, and for what she came to be as an adult: a stunning beauty, an accomplished artist, a natural leader and organizer giving freely of her time to her community. She loved to dance, she could sing, she could write (as the e-mails attest), she was the consummate hostess, a miracle worker in the kitchen and, as John would acknowledge to a very few close friends, a wife and lover beyond dreams. On top of this she was one of the kindest persons ever, never a harsh word to or about anyone, with a smile that would stop trains, as John would often say.

Their story, as seventy-somethings in the mid-2000s, begins with their long-ago classmates from that same grade school in the midst of the 1930's Great Depression. Most of these grade schoolers went through the system to high school graduation or beyond and became a rather remarkably close-knit group. They stuck together, enjoyed their every-five-years class reunions and made a habit of lunching together once a month, first Thursday, at a local I-Hop restaurant.

Joan, widowed after 52 years of marriage to a successful health insurance broker, and feeling the loneliness, sought out old friends who had known her as a school chum years before. She had been a popular student, by most accounts the prettiest girl in school, but her social life during the World War II years was limited by her obligations at home, caring for her "baby" brother, eight years her junior. Her mother worked, in order to keep up the life insurance premiums for Joan's father, while he, a surgeon, was commanding a military field hospital overseas. An Army Medical Corps captain, he went ashore at Normandy, France, in June 1944 on D-Day plus One, picking up the pieces of the American dead and knitting back together those for whom it was possible to do so.

John, too, began going to those class luncheons when his work permitted. He and Joan had dated several times in college, but by then they were committed to others. John never had asked Joan for a date in high school. He was at that time a typically inept-with-girls teen and his ineptness persuaded him that Joan would most likely turn him down. And because his admiration for Joan was so great, he could not risk the humiliation of rejection. And so he never asked.

Nonetheless, John and Joan remained good friends throughout their adult years, Joan never imagining John's longstanding love for her in his heart. They worked together on class reunions, built a class mailing list, and were comfortable with their occasional connections.

It was about this time that John had one of those powerful dreams—for him, rare—a vision he later thought. He was in his early 70s and in his sleep he saw Joan, in a stunning yellow knee-length dress, walking down the Opernstrasse Ring Road in Vienna, Austria, a city he had visited some years earlier. Her gait was visibly "regal," as he would later write to her about his vision. (Joan had excellent posture, directed by her father at an early age at the family dining table. Dad would walk around the table, poking his three daughters between the shoulders, demanding that they "sit straight.") In the vision, John was on a Viennese Ring Road streetcar and there, off to the left on the broad boulevard sidewalk, was Joan, striding purposefully ahead, regally. The streetcar stopped at an intersection, John could see that Joan was crossing in front of the stopped car. He jumped off, followed her as best he could into the women's boutique she had just entered. John entered too but could not find her. He awoke at that moment with a huge sense of disappointment, of loss.

On thinking about it, John accepted this "vision" experience—perhaps a premonition of some kind—as a powerful reminder of how much Joan had been in his sub-conscious for such a very long time.

Their e-mail exchanges began in February 2005, shortly after John, then 75, had been diagnosed with bladder cancer. He shared that information with his classmates at their February luncheon—Joan was present—describing the urologist's prognosis with a light touch. If he was scared to death he tried not to show it. A few days later he received this e-mail from Joan, an unexpected but beautiful surprise: "His" Joan had noticed, and *cared*!

CHAPTER 1

Beginnings

2-8-05

My dear friend,

You were a cool cat heading for your cancer news that day at the luncheon. I admire the humorous, light hearted reasons you suggested as explanation. It is a good attitude. But I have been told three different times that I had cancer, and I know the emotions that go on inside every time.

I am a pray-er. I wrote that without the hyphen and it didn't sound right. My computer doesn't like my spelling, but I don't care. I am part of a cancer support group at my church. We are assigned an individual with cancer, or more than one sometimes, to pray for twice a week for three months. That person does not know who is praying, only that it is being done. For you I will pray daily, and you can be sure it is being done. I will include prayer for the skills of Drs. Kevin Ward, Jonathan Moceri and the others who attend you.

Faith, Strength, Courage, Comfort, Hope, and Healing,

Love, Joan

As it happened, John's bladder cancer was controlled by surgery and chemo treatments and he was able to resume, gradually, a near-normal lifestyle. That one e-mail from Joan had had a more therapeutic effect, he thought later, than all the doctoring he could imagine. He wanted to talk to Joan more often than once a month at their class luncheons and he suggested, via e-mail, that they might be able to meet face to face before the next gathering. They lived only a few miles distant from each other at that time, but John's opportunities to visit Joan were limited, owing to his unusual working environment.

3-9
Hello again,

Tomorrow I should be home all day, but I'm not a morning person, especially if I don't have an early commitment. Mondays, Wednesdays and Fridays I leave the house at nine. Other days anytime from nine till noon is o.k. unless I'm playing bridge, going to a meeting etc. Don't give up. We'll Talk.

John's response to this brief but encouraging e-mail led him to suggest a getting-to-know-you exchange. It had been 55 years since they dated in college and he had no idea what Joan's widowed world was really like. Unfortunately, his e-mail back to Joan has been lost but he remembers asking her "what-about-you?" questions in an early-morning e-mail: Her responses tell us about this:

CHAPTER 2

Getting to Know You

3-14
You do get up early. I can't give answers without elaborating in most cases, but I'll try to be brief.

Daily newspaper: The King County Journal. I used to take the P. I. too, because I wanted the contrast of the most far left and most conservative local papers. I kept throwing unread papers away, because I couldn't find time. I take the Mercer Island Reporter, a weekly, for little town news and obits. No magazines. Periodically, I have taken the New York Times.

Light reading: A variety. I used to like Dominick Dunne and John Grisham. I read Anne Tyler, Rosamunde Pilcher, and other women novelists. It is not so light but I am, and have been for ages, reading John Adams, which I love. Two favorite books have been Stephen Ambrose, Undaunted Courage and David Horowitz, Radical Son. Those weren't so light either. Problem is, for the past two years I haven't been able to concentrate enough on reading. Most recent novel: If it was a novel, The No. 1 Ladies Detective Agency by Alexander McCall Smith. It takes place in Botswana, Africa. Fun.

Favorite color: Yellow. I don't wear, it but it makes me feel like sunshine.

Radio listening. I wake up to Kirby Wilbur. He's not my favorite, but the time is right. Tony Snow is my favorite, Rush is second, used to be first. I sometimes hear Michael Medved, John Carlson, all the conservatives. I like to listen to smooth jazz, even if it is on NPR. It is available on other stations, too.

Gardening: This could take a long time. Yes. My property is about 60% of an acre and is part of an old orchard. When we moved here, there were 12 apple trees and a pear tree. I've added a pie cherry, and three of the apples have bit the dust. Since 1966 when we built the house, I have pruned all those trees annually, except for last year when my wonderful neighbors helped with a couple. This year they did five, and I did five. Last year I had 80 containers on my deck, and around the front entrance. Many of them were things like tomatoes in boxes, and herbs in pots under my kitchen window, lots of red geraniums etc. etc. I live on a very hilly property. It is a pretty casual garden, but much a part of my life.

TV: Fox News. I search for the now seldom good plays, or new Television "movies." It is pretty sparse. When I find them I get DVDs of fairly current movies. When I just want to have mindless relaxation in the evening, I watch Dr. Phil or Oprah.

Favorite Flower: I love them all and always have some in my house. I think simple cheerful daisies have always come in first.

Now it is your turn. Answer the questions on your test.

Your friend, Joan

That Joan called John's questions a "test," suggested a certain impishness in her personality. He loved it and could hardly wait to respond.

At that time, John was engaged in a sensitive U.S. Government project, located near Seattle. While it was difficult for him to get away from his office for more than an hour or so, he was able to telephone Joan, knowing that she probably would be at home at the time of his call. He phoned her, for the first time, and they talked for nearly an hour, Joan relating the highlights of her World War II experiences as a very young teenager. His notes and e-mail response:

Tuesday evening (3-15) (sent Wed a.m., 8:45)

Joan:

If I weren't so furious with myself I would probably cry.

I've been keeping our e-mail correspondence since the February luncheon on my office computer—which technically is a no-no (Uncle Sam, you see)—and in a password-protected file, safe and easy to use. But just now, when trying to add to that file your responses to my "test," I zapped the whole thing. Even the trash bin didn't catch it, owing to another boner of mine. Fortunately your "answers" are safe but I'll really miss re-reading your wonderful words about prayer and encouragement, and your other notes as well. As Henry Higgins sang, "Damn, damn, damn, I've grown accustomed to—"

My mind still spins as I digest what you told me this morning about your family's WW II struggles. And shame on you if you haven't yet got round to writing all that down for your grandchildren. Don't deny them that. I'll have a few more questions about that saga when I phone next.

Lastly, don't worry about brevity. Everything you send goes into a word processor. You write beautifully and I enjoy every word.

More later as I get to it, but this exchange of "tests" is no substitute for our having lunch together. I would like that.

Yr *old* (deteriorating?) friend, John

From John to Joan, Sent 9 p.m. 3-17

Randomly:

You're a much deeper/wider reader than I. For fiction I do mostly Clancy, Ludlum, Grisham and Crighton. I think I've read everything they've done. And as an old foreign affairs junkie, and with the job I have now, I read a lot of international stuff on-line, especially on the ME, South Asia and Islamist terrorism generally, much of it on the Web in English-language pages from all over the world. I subscribe to *Commentary* and *The Weekly Standard*, the latter, by the way, you would enjoy very much. It's the conservative answer—sort of, not so much straight news—to Time, Newsweek, etc., edited by Bill Kristol. It's neo-con in outlook, a blend I much admire, ditto *Commentary*.

Medved, as you know, is a converted liberal Jewish-American, and a neighbor of Mercer Island's Rabbi Daniel Lapin, who are wonderful champions of conservative Christianity in America. If you don't know it, you can be proud of your very own local Jewish-American patriots! I love 'em both and listen when I can.

Color, blue; flower, probably gladiolus although I've rarely tried to grow them. Daffodils/tulips would be a close second, sentiment from the '40s grunt labor in our Puyallup Valley bulb fields. Regarding yellow for you: I grant that you know best, but you sure were stunning in that yellow dress on the Viennese boulevard! Of course in my vision your hair was still that beautiful dark brown that I remember so well from 1950 and back to first grade! And the yellow dress—well, you get the idea!

Movies. Of the WW II genre, no doubt Saving Private Ryan and The Longest Day. My ambassador in Moscow was a good friend of the latter's author, Cornelius Ryan, who visited there and talked to our embassy staff about the book/movie. Your words on the phone reminded me of that scene at the end of the Ryan movie, at the U.S. memorial cemetery at Normandy, which still chokes me up when now-old-guy Ryan says "I just wanted to be worthy." Thinking of your dad wading ashore through all that carnage on D-Day Plus One makes me tear up as I type this. If you ever go to Normandy be sure to see Saving Ryan beforehand, if you haven't yet.

"Peaceful" movies: the Harrison/Hepburn version of My Fair Lady is my all-time favorite although I wish Audrey's lip-synching had been closer to perfect. And I've enjoyed most of Harrison Ford's stuff, especially his parts in Clancy's movies. Another would be The Russia House, Michelle Pfeiffer's portrayal of Katya was outstanding, I thought, her English-Russian accent unbelievably authentic. Sean Connery, finally an older man, was great, too.

Radio: Rarely on at home, except when I'm eating lunch alone, then Medved. Up to the bladder surgery I was going 3x/week to Balley Fitness for ½ hr workout and listened most to Kirby, sometimes to Mike Siegel, depending on topic. Like you, I think I may now prefer Tony to Rush, but again it depends on what they're talking about. My trip home every Tuesday morning after bible study assures some time with them every week. Otherwise it's spotty, depends on time of day in car, but usually between KTTH and KVI. Maybe you could steer me toward some good jazz, I've never really tried.

I suspect your hilly property helps explain why you are in such good shape. But be very careful with ladders, as you probably are. My first ladder fall happened last summer, from "only" four feet off the ground, cracked a rib and slowed me down for weeks. It *can* happen.

My "garden" is small, a bird sanctuary mainly, built it myself ten years ago, just off the deck to my bachelor pad, has a small pond and several water courses, self-contained pump system, some small "Alpine" trees and evergreen shrubs for bird cover. I have no green thumb, however, as you obviously do. Bring some pictures next time, if you can.

TV. Almost only pro baseball and football. I enjoyed The Practice but find its Boston Legal successor too much a skin flick, even though I like Candice Bergen (not her politics, of course). The occasional PBS documentary is okay, recently a long piece on the al-Saud family was accurate and fascinating. Old movies are another story, I like many of them from our post-WWII days, although I must admit the acting today is a lot better.

Friend John

3-18, 10:30 a.m.
Could I resend the information you lost? I hate to see you cry.

As to reading, I don't know Ludlum and Crighton. I do know Bill Kristol from T.V. but have never read his magazine.

Cliff joined Daniel Lapin's "Toward Tradition" Jewish/Christian Conservative Organization long ago. I still pay the dues and receive their newsletter. I, too, admire both Lapin and Medved and feel good about the unity they project with the Christian faith. Mercer Island has a large percentage of Jews. My daughter in law's father is Jewish. It is nearly impossible to live on Mercer Island without having Jewish friends, and I have quite a few.

Blue was the color I would have guessed for you. Any of us kids who spent Spring gazing at daffodils and tulips in the Puyallup Valley, with Mt. Rainier out there in the distance, must be forever influenced by that scene. I remember sitting in the swing on our weeping willow tree and swinging out to look over those yellow fields below. Maybe that's why yellow is my favorite.

Your garden sounds great. You must have worked hard to put it together. I'm for birds, too, and have a lot because of fruit trees, blueberries, which we fight over, and the cherries. I have a bird bath which was really funny last summer when I saw two huge crows in it. I tried to take a picture, but they flew away too soon. Later I did a water color painting of that scene, from memory. I never quite finished it but I like it and look at it often. We used to have lots of quail. I used them as subjects for many batik "pictures" which I was turning out at the time. It breaks my heart that there are none left on the Island.

Your friend for 70 years,

Joan

Sent a.m. 3-19
Subject: Fuzzy Sunshine
Click on the attached icon

Hi,
This isn't a very good photograph, but hey:

1. It's yellow, as in Sunshine
2. It's for you
3. It's my first-ever digital picture.

Great buy at Costco, 4.0 megapixels for 200 bucks, Olympus, no less. I've needed one for some time now, if only to become modern, but I sure need practice!

3-19, Morning
(Subject: Not so fuzzy)
What a nice way to start the day. Thanks.

I wandered lonely as a cloud
That floats on high o'r vales and hills,
When all at once I saw a crowd,
A host of golden daffodils
Beside the lake, beneath the trees,
Fluttering and dancing in the breeze.

It seems to me we had to memorize that poem of Wordsworth in a Junior High lit class. You were in the same class—you ought to know it. I can't remember all the words now, but I think of it every Spring. Your picture inspired me to get out a poetry book and read it all.

I printed the picture and it looks good to me.

Sent 3:20 p.m. Sun 3-20
Hi,

Wordsworth? You're amazing! As I began to read it I knew instantly I'd memorized it at one time, somewhere in the Sumner school system, your recollection is surely correct.

More later,

Your friend

Sent 7 p.m., 3-20

I guess we could take turns "talking" about things of mutual interest, you don't have to wait for me to do the quizzing.

E.g., great church service today, (my job *does* let me out on Sundays!) in which I was privileged to participate. I read from the lectern every 4th or 5th Sunday, OT and NT scriptures. Thought of you during the service, wondering as I have before: When/how did you get into the church "habit"? Do you have favorite TV preachers to listen to when you don't feel like going? Are you in charge of that cancer prayer program? How many of you do it? Besides choir (a big job, I know), any other extracurricular things?

We just finished a six-part study of The Revelation, first time at our church in years. Very, very good, and different!

In recent years I've come to appreciate Holy Week very much. I hope you do, too, and that this will be a very good seven days for you.

God bless.

Sent a.m. 3-21
Almost forgot. If you're willing to re-send a couple of those earlier messages, that would be great. The one with "cool cat" in the text is one, the other is your weekly routine. Thanks loads.

Rec'd early a.m. 3-22, written 11 p.m. nite before

John,

It is late. Your questions leave me in the process of writing my life story. I've nearly filled one page. Strange how questions stir up thoughts and memories. I'll work on it more later on. And I will send duplicates of lost words later too. 'Bye for now. Joan

Sent early a.m. 3-22, after above.
Wow, you and I need to get our clocks in better synch. I'm reading your note at 5 a.m., having gone to bed at 9:30 wondering if I'd turned you off with e-mail overload.

Phonecon Tues 3-22, 10:45 a.m. She had not read your e-mail and had a doctor's appointment at 11:30 so we couldn't meet. She said "I would have said yes—" (but for the doctor thing). She says she hopes it's not serious. I told her I'd pray for a good outcome. Great review of her mom's handling the family during the war, how she met husband Cliff (blind date in 1950—need to pin this down, whether they were already dating when I took her out, the BIG question). He was two years older than she, joined Marines before end of WWII but never went overseas. Back to college in an Army ROTC unit but he volunteered for Korea, not waiting for his outfit to be called up. Details about her accident with a logging truck, no one hurt but she didn't drive afterward until age 34! She was fined by a local judge who apparently pocketed the money. Should ask her to complete the story of Cliff's service.

John's note to himself:

That phone call has a lesson for you: She seems comfortable with this relationship, not offended by your eagerness which you surely feel a lot more than she does. So stop torturing yourself with worry when she doesn't respond immediately. And any *simple*, spontaneous get-together is likely to work if she has time and ample warning. You haven't dated anyone for so long you've forgotten how to be cool, and this, after all, is *Joan*, not just anybody!

Also: Given opportunity, she's a talker and it's possible (likely) you're a rare (only?) willing ear available to her these days. That's exactly what this kind of friendship ought to do, give her opportunities to feel better about whatever is on her mind.

CHAPTER 3

John's Love Story

Sent 3:50 p.m., 3-22-05

My Story (most of it)

Dearest friend,

This is going to be too long and, for me, difficult, maybe for you too. I have to try to slip you into my moccasins for a few minutes, not so easy.

I go back to the e-mail Geneve sent me (I was in Arizona at the time) when she heard that Cliff had died—earlier she had told me he was very ill—and my reaction to that. I was terribly saddened and immediately very worried about you. I vowed then to do whatever I could—obvious to me, limited, because of geography and my work at the time—to try to take some of the sting out of your pain. At that time I didn't know that you, too, are a believer.

Joan, you couldn't possibly remember it after all these years, how I tried to get your attention, but even at age six I saw something very special in you, more than just playground stuff, and I fell in love with you.

Most guys get over this kind of feeling, I never did. Even at the UW, my (eventual) wife Colleen knew about you, that she was "second choice." But we were "even" on that score because I was second to her "first," a Chi Psi who was killed in Korea. Point is that Colleen knew that I had been in love with you for a very long time, a kind of permanent state of heart. Today, of course, I like to think that that love has matured to *agapeo*, if you know your NT Greek a little bit, the kind that Christians are supposed to have for each other as expression of God's presence in our lives. About you it's a little more complicated than that, very special because of our history and my feelings for you over all these years. There have been very few weeks that have passed from 1951 onward that I didn't think about you, good thoughts about your well being, good marriage, fine kids, comfort, safety, all that. Then, much later, when I learned about Jesus and how to pray, my prayers were along the same lines.

When I wrote you about that incredible "Vienna" dream (more like a vision, actually)—Cliff was still alive—I may have fibbed by saying that I hadn't thought about you in some time. I didn't want to admit it then, that you were never far from my mind, too complicated for a happily married woman to absorb, certainly for Cliff if you chose to share the story with him.

What scares me a bit, the idea goes something like this: If an impartial shrink were to talk to both of us, separately, about our friendship, he would likely conclude that I need it a lot more than you do. That would be bad because I'm the one who's supposed to be supportive, the human outlet for God's love, man helping (widowed) woman as Scripture commands. But I confess I've never had a friendship like this and the thought of losing it, frankly, is quite troubling. That you are one of a very few who know about my professional background as a CIA officer—and this sort of goofy job I have right now—is more important to me than you can know, so there's lots to talk about that doesn't go very well on the telephone: all the shared history, the huge gaps to fill, and your present-and-future. Not to mention your talents, avocations and, yes, your politics!

There's a bit more to this story, which I probably won't put in writing, but which you're entitled to know to round out the picture. I'm pretty sure I'll be able to talk about that, and soon!

I hope this wasn't too much. You are *so special*, please know that.

Your friend, John

Sent a.m. 4-23
John, I am overwhelmed. You can't possibly know the emotions that are swirling through my brain. Thank you for giving me the gift of your friendship. It is fun to exchange thoughts and ideas and to discover that we have lots in common. It is generous of you to tell me all those things, and I feel affirmed and blessed that you are a part of my life.

Holy Week is important to me too. Tomorrow night the choir will practice. Friday night we will sing at the evening service. Sunday at 8:45 a.m. we practice. We sing at 9:30 and again at 11:00. Our anthem will be the Widor "Festival Alleluias." It is the song with which we ended every concert in England and Scotland last year. The following week we are going to do the "Hallelujah Chorus." I am still struggling to learn that. In the evening, I will be having Easter Dinner at my house for family members, my sister Barbara, my nieces, my great nieces, my daughter Libby, and possibly an appearance by my son and his girl friend. Easter will be a busy and joyful day.

Have a wonderful week.

Joan

Also, same time:

Monday is a busy day. After my hours at church I came home to pay a bunch of bills and get my income tax in the mail. In answer to your requests, yes, I will re-send those e-mails you requested, but not right now because I have to type them over unless there is a secret way to send them from the SENT file. I have no idea what computers are capable of doing or not doing.

Of course, I am curious about many things about your life. You can explain how YOU got the church habit. My parents did not go to church. They dropped us kids at Sunday school, probably rather sporadically. My dad always had hospital rounds to do on Sunday mornings, or that was the excuse.

I think I believed right from the start. Did you go to that Sunday school in Sumner's big brown Presbyterian Church? I can't remember. I went to church off and on by choice through my teen years . . . . Always went to the Sunrise Service up on the hill early Easter morning, usually with girl friends when we were teenagers.

I walked to church with my sisters or alone from time to time. When I got to the UW I investigated Catholicism and went to some classes the church gave. When Cliff went overseas soon after we were married, I went every Sunday to church. I prayed every day. Every Sunday I shook the Pastor's hand. No one ever asked me to be a part of anything to do with that church. It was disappointing. But God helped me through that scary time.

When Cliff came home from Korea, we moved to Seattle to finish school. No church. We moved to Mercer Island two years later and started trying different churches. Finally, when I was 27, we joined Mercer Island Presbyterian. It was a fledgling church, three years old with only Sunday School rooms and a Fellowship Hall. I was baptized there. We were faithful worshipers and participated in some of the activities, but during the time of the turmoil of the sixties Cliff began to feel the church was sympathetic to Communism and refused to let his children go to Sunday school. We stopped going too.

At about the time I was in my early forties, our twelve year old son became a serious problem. I needed God. So I started back to church. Cliff followed soon after, and we scarcely missed a

Sunday after that. I went to weekly Bible Study and sometimes did volunteer Jobs. Now I do Choir, lead the exercise class, go to Bible Study, sometimes arrange flowers for Sunday, fill in for the receptionist during lunch on Mondays, pray for cancer patients (no I don't run that committee) and occasionally help with one-time projects.

Reading this over I see that I have done what many people do. We move toward God and then back off from time to time. It has been a long time since I backed off. I've had some remarkable experiences to strengthen my faith.

Sent a.m. 3-23
Joan,
No, don't bother to re-type them. If you highlight an item in your In Box, there should then be a "forward" button somewhere near the top of your screen, just click on that and follow whatever other commands follow. It's ultra simple once you see how it works.

So much to reflect on, but my writing team is up against another deadline and so I'll have to wait a bit. Your Easter should be beautiful, I'm really glad about that.

Thanks for hearing me out with that first part of My Story. I feel a great weight lifted, of very long duration.

On Easter, after church, I will be driving to Forks with an old Russian specialist from Boston. We have been to Kamchatka together, in 1997 and 98, working on an international fisheries research project (wild steelhead trout). Now we fish together on the Olympic Peninsula every late March, for about a week. I will sorely miss our "chats," but wanted you to know. I'll be back on line April 3, you can "stand down" until then. If I can I'll try to reach you by cell, but please don't alter your schedule in anticipation of this as it's pretty uncertain as of now.

Why not say it, Joan: I love you (but you know that).

CHAPTER 4

Holy Week

As I've said, you probably don't remember my trying to tug at your pigtails in that Sumner Presbyterian Sunday School. I'm sure we were there together, and just as sure that's what I would have tried to do, anything to get your attention! I do remember that I went occasionally with my mom, kicking and screaming all the way.

Intelligence officers are not only supposed to be apolitical but many of them actually are irreligious. I was a huge skeptic in my 20s and 30s, because most of my (Ivy League) colleagues were, and to the extent we talked about faith (rarely), they persuasively spoke about fairy tales, etc.

Most of my faith story as an adult is all wound up in my effort to save my marriage to Colleen, but I failed. It's another one of those things I'm hoping we can talk about some day.

Hey, gal, I'm going to give you a break, so you can focus on Easter at home. I can receive e-mail until Saturday evening but if I don't hear from you I'll know why. Our focus these past weeks has been a bit unusual, on each other, let's zero in on Him for the rest of the week!! ILY

Sent 7:30 p.m., 3-23

How could I forget. Re your doctor's visit, how to focus my prayers: Concern, thanksgiving, okay? Not nosey, concerned.

Friend

John's note to himself:

Phonecon morning 3-23 she describes reasons for her doc's appointment yesterday. Some months ago she awoke in the dark, stood up and fell over, scared to death. Called 911. They came and couldn't find anything wrong. Tests followed. She has high bp but has known about this for years, taking regular meds for it. This is a balance, light-headedness problem, possibly inner-ear related. (Sounds an awful lot like my own symptoms.) They're doing a carotid artery test, maybe an MRI (?). She's very concerned about stroke as that is what took both her parents. Mom lingered for several years thru many small strokes, in J's home. Her dad didn't last very long after the first one. So your prayers can be very specific.

Sent evening 3-24
I promised I wouldn't bug you any more this week, but—

For something different, I drove down to Sumner Pres, knowing they were to do a performance of Leonardo's "Last Supper." Twelve disciples plus Jesus, many of whom I knew from days past, all just guys in the church, super job of acting by each, describing their individual roles in Jesus' life. Powerful, emotional, convicting. You would have been proud of your (our) old church and I would have squeezed your hand if you'd been there beside me!!

Apropos of that Maundy Thursday service, Rex Weick's widow was there. You probably remember him, he ran the local grocery for years during the 30s 40s and 50s. Rex, along with your dad, were "the most handsome men in town," according to my mother's unassailable opinion. She thought the same of your mom, hands down "Sumner's Most Beautiful Woman," so it never surprised me that you were always the prettiest girl in school.

Again, a joyous Easter! He is risen indeed!!

Sent a.m. 3-26

John,

You do remind me of the old days in Sumner, familiar names and places. It also tickles me to hear your descriptive comments about your mom's personality. I didn't really know her, but she sounds like a strong woman with definite opinions.

I missed Maundy Thursday service at my church. After Wednesday night Choir practice, knowing that Good Friday night we started at 6:30 and wouldn't be through till 8:30, I decided to miss it. I am going to go out to dinner with Libby and then to the theater to see a new musical on Saturday night. Sunday is choir practice at 8:45 followed by two services. YOUR service on Thursday sounded rewarding.

Surprise! I got a piece of mail from you today. You had mentioned being involved with salmon in Russia. I had no idea how involved, nor had I ever heard of Kamchatka. The pictures are beautiful and it must be a fisherman's unspoiled paradise. You will have to continue the story. Alaska, I know a little about. I've only spent 48 hours there, in and around Anchorage, but Cliff spent ten years doing business in Alaska, six weeks there, then six weeks home, that's half of each year. He did some fishing, spent a lot of time on those float planes, once got dropped off in a wilderness with some buddies, no lodges, organized camp or anything. Bears came in and did away with lots of stuff while they were fishing. Obviously things have improved a lot . . . and have become a lot more expensive than way back then which was probably 1955 to 1965. My son worked two winters on a crab packing boat in Dutch Harbor when he was 18 and 19.

Have fun on your fishing trip. I hope you catch some, but I know that fishing isn't only about catching fish. It sometimes is about camaraderie, always about challenges, communion with nature, and solace for the soul. You are rewarded even when you don't catch a thing. Take your rain gear and have a safe journey.

3-29 Tues after Easter, cell phonecon from downtown Forks, John's notes:

Great support from church member/friends at time of Cliff's at-home illness. Lots of help at home Easter Sunday, family members brought stuff, helped w/ cleanup but she was pooped Monday a.m.

Talked about 30 minutes, very relaxed, friendly. She appreciated the call from the river bank yesterday although she chided mildly that I didn't give her enough time to really hear the river. I had held the cell phone close to the riffling surface, a sound that always lulls me, but apparently it didn't pick up well enough for her to hear it. Darn!!

Cliff went to Alaska for his company, had to travel all over the country, signing up clients. She was in her mid-20s at this time. He got very tired of it and on his last trip took her to Anchorage. This included a flyover of a nearby bay in which they spotted a huge pod of white whales, something she remembers as a real highlight.

She joined her church about 4 yrs after it opened, has since been active in many of its ministries: bible study participant (not leader, apparently), flower arranging, choir (did she used to solo?), prayer support program. Church has huge physical plant, including gym (used for largest gatherings), classrooms, many others. Three services on Sunday, and (I think) evening weekday services as well.

3-30, about 4 p.m. phonecon: Nice long chat. Said she's "very serious" about learning about my family, work, marriage, etc., "we'll have a lot to talk about." Anent the idea of a hospital visit, she allowed as to how she normally insists on makeup and hair-do but in such a situation would very much appreciate a visit—from you.

Another doc appointment last day or so, all seems okay w/ the balance problem. Got her hearing checked first time ever, it's okay.

When I asked if she and her two sisters are singers we got into a chat about college singing. That led to learning that she pledged Alpha Phi as a frosh in '47 (!!!). She said "you weren't around much" (understatement of my life). She thinks our one date was in the summer "because I was quite tan," (why would she remember that—special dress, etc.?) but couldn't put a year on it. She quit school in Jr year and came back to graduate in '53 (Cliff is now in picture, he went off to ski in Idaho for awhile).

I think she's as eager as I am for some face-to-face conversation.

I sent this about 5 p.m. Sat. evening, Apr 2

Hi,

I drafted this on my laptop before our phone conversation Wednesday afternoon, but I'll leave most of it as it was.

As I said on the phone yesterday, no way was I going to go eight days without "communicating."

You sure know how to buckle a guy's knees, as when you said to me, "you were never around much," *and* after I had just learned that you pledged Alphi Phi in Fall '47 as a frosh. That meant that you and I, in two separate buildings, lived within 300 yards (or less) of each other for the better part of three years, and I must have been totally unaware until the social exchange between our two houses that brought you back into view. (I need recall help on that, also—a little "down memory lane" rehashing.) I'm trying to imagine how this could have been and conclude it was your move to Tacoma for your senior HS year when you dropped off my screen—until our two dates at the U-W. Much more on that later, for sure. Well, back to the pre-phonecon note:

A couple of ideas in my mind, from our earlier phone call in which you told me about your health concerns. God forbid it should happen, but if you were to suddenly wind up in a hospital or a nursing home or somewhere else out of reach, I'd sure like to know about it asap. And unless you're the type who has to have full makeup and hair-do for visitors, I would want to come visit, even if for five minutes. Really. So be thinking about whom (Libby, Barbara, whoever) you might ask to reach me in such a situation, ahead of time, "just in case."

By the way, and this could be important, now that I know you would do this via Libby: I know you know her well, but it is still important that in no way does she ever think I'm trying to compete for the memory of her dad. Some children quite naturally resent the presence of another man in Mom's life, after Dad has gone. I don't need to tell you this, but on the other hand let's not overlook the possibility.

Another idea, more pleasant to contemplate: Next time you're near your post office, why not swing in there and take a look around for a nearby coffee shop or restaurant or anyplace else that would accommodate some low-key conversation. I can find the MI P.O. without difficulty but I have no clue about what's nearby. I may have spur-of-the-moment opportunities, from time to time, to break out of this office routine for a couple of hours and it would be nice to know of a place or two that we could go to without spending a lot of time/uncertainty getting there.

Today (Wednesday) I fished only in the morning, kind of tired me as the stamina isn't yet back to full normal and the high-water wading exacerbates the internal bleeding (which is normal, Doc insists). So this afternoon I have the house to myself. Brought along the instructional CD for the new digital camera which I'll plug in as soon as I finish this note. I'm also working on a pair of slightly-leaking waders, so there's plenty to do with my free afternoon.

One of my two friends hooked a fish this morning but it was off instantly. First action we've had, rivers are all too high but we're trying. The fisher I speak of, Pete Soverel, is one of the world's best steelhead flyfishers, acknowledged among the fraternity as such, so it's a real pleasure and privilege to watch him at work. He was on President Reagan's White House staff in the '80s, Annapolis grad, decorated Vietnam vet, headed the U-Dub NROTC program (as a Navy captain) for a few years, is now a part-time prof there at the Jackson School, teaches strategy/tactics and war. I'll tell you more about him when we get some time to ourselves. He's the one who has taken "my" 1993 Kamchatka project and made it into a $6 million/year program, amazing guy.

Gotta go. Thanks for bearing with me! Love you.

PS (Fri): Tried to phone Thursday afternoon, I think I left a msg on your answering service. No opportunities today. I plan to send this off by e-mail sometime before bed Saturday, when I'll get home. Since that Wednesday shock talk (your first two years at the U-Dub) my mind has been All Joan All Day All The Time!! But *we'll* fix it. I just need patience.

'Bye

4-2—10 p.m. Saturday

Hi,

It is good to connect. Both times you called to no avail, I was on the phone. The first time if it had been about two minutes later I could have answered. Today I was in an overly long conversation with an old friend and neighbor whom I hadn't heard from for a very long time. She talked for over an hour and a half. I kept thinking you might be trying. Sure enough. I checked when she hung up, and there was your message. It is eleven p.m. now on daylight savings time. I set the clocks ahead early, so I am sure to get to church in plenty of time to practice for the Hallelujah Chorus.

Libby will be here tomorrow to do her laundry. She knows we keep in touch. I plan to ask her to let you know early on if I have any sudden health problem that I can't tell you myself. She knows that you keep track of all the '47 class friends and send e-mails to let everyone know when one of us needs prayers, birthday greetings, hospital visits etc. No problem.

It did occur to me that your chemo treatments may lower your energy level, not as good as usual for a fishing trip. The weather didn't make it any easier either. I am glad you are safely home.

I have to get a little sleep now.

Goodnight, John

Phonecon after John's return from Forks:

We talked for 1-1/2 hrs! Highlights:

Need to cover further the social exchange between your two houses that re-surfaced her. She quit the sorority end of Jr year because they threatened to campus her for the whole spring quarter for being "a little bit wicked" (follow this) but she was part of a group, all the rest of whom were townies who suffered not at all. She gave her pin back and left. Worked at Rhodes in Tacoma (while living w/ folks), decorated store windows and did other art work for them. So she met Cliff during later part of Jr year, on blind date, but nothing got serious until after she had been away from school for awhile. So your date w/ her was spring qtr Jr year after you and Colleen were already pretty tight. Boy, to live that over again!

Few groups about Cliff's business in connection with her late dinner habit. She eats between 8 and 9, growing out of his habit of dealing with clients in bars over drinks and coming home late most evenings.

She welcomes idea of spending time w/ you, driving around, showing places, maybe even into her home. She has already collected photos of her art work and garden to show you and is just waiting for face-to-face opportunity, so you need to break away from all this office stuff and get over there!

She plays bridge w/ several groups, often on Tuesdays and Thursdays, either a.m. or after lunch. But don't worry about phoning on these days, her least busy. If she has company, she'll say so and you won't cause problems. And phoning any evening but Thursday (choir practice) is okay, esp between eight and nine when she'll probably be eating. She is always up until 11 or later. Gets up as late as her day allows, but usually by 8:30. Her e-mail to you this morning was sent at 7:30 a.m.

Beginning sometime in May she's going to be very busy with the Bellevue Arts Museum, of whose guild she is the secretary. The guild sponsors an art fair every year in Bellevue and raises about $1m each time for the museum. It's been closed for awhile for renovation and this spring/summer is going to be a big deal. So you should figure out a way to get over there before mid-May.

Her dad was indeed a fast driver. Bought a '48 Buick (new) after he'd set up practice in Tacoma, piled the whole family into it (four kids, himself and wife)

25

and somewhere on U.S. 10 in E. Wash decided to see if it would do 120 mph as advertised. It did, scared everyone to death. He had many speeding tickets during his career. Tried to teach J how to drive but barked at her too much, she never did get it. This may have had something to do with her crash on their honeymoon.

Her mom worked at the canary during WWII as a "stenographer," office helper. J went to her office only once, to ask permission to join her friends on a swimming trip to Surprise Lake. Mom thought J was bringing bad news about her dad and her mom really lit into her, telling her never to come to the office again.

J was pretty much tied down by her mom during her hs years. She went to the rec hall a few times, remembers dancing with me (?—I think that's what she said) but her social life (implied) was much cut down by her responsibilities for young Alex. Follow this up: it looks as though, by her own measure, she had a pretty limited and not-very-fulfilling social life through all of hs. Ask her about this, college, too, and whether she was expecting anything from you after her dad's encouragement that she "look you over."

Sent 6 a.m., Tue 4-5.

It's 0530 (that's CIA/military time, I'm sure Cliff used it occasionally) Tuesday and my office prep time. (I also do a little bible reading at this hour.) Another of those eerie coincidences as I'm thanking God for your incredible openness with me last night on the phone as you shared your pain over all those years. I'm reading the last part of Jesus' Sermon on the Mount and especially Mt 7:7-11 where we are encouraged to pray about *all things.* That I can now do much better, thanks to your willingness to share. Thank you!

God bless.

Sent noon 4-6, after worrying about her silence for more than 24 hrs!

Hi,
Noon, Wed.

Quickly, I have the whole afternoon available, unexpectedly of course.

Trying to reach you by phone, knowing it's an awful long shot.

PS: Chemo, just completed, seems to have been a breeze. I'm feeling fine, maybe even a little frisky. Your prayers sure helped in the run-up, however. I was pretty nervous.

12:10 response:
John,

I was on the phone and picked up your message a couple of minutes after you sent it. You sounded exasperated. I felt that way, too. I'm glad the chemo went well. I'll be here all day if you have anything else to say.

Joan

CHAPTER 5

Finally, Alone Together

John had Mariners tickets for an afternoon game with the Minnesota Twins but he feels guilty about leaving his cooped-up writing team during a work day. Even so, instead of baseball he goes directly to Joan's home, where they visit for three hours. Months later, Joan told him about that afternoon meeting. He had taken her by the hand and helped her climb the hilly slope up into her orchard. At that moment she said to herself, "This (with John) is where I belong."

John explained to Joan why he was concerned about Joan's telling others about their relationship. His job was a very sensitive one and he was using a cover story to account to friends for his activities during his 12-month contract. He told Joan that the decision was hers to make, but rather than trying to explain "just who is this guy?" to friends and family it might be easier for her simply to not talk about it. Joan agreed that, at least for the time being, "mum's the word."
The next morning:

8 a.m. 4-7
Good Morning,

I'm glad we talked about my cover story problem. You are so guileless, Joan, and I don't want you to have to change *anything* in your being, on my account. I think we both know you made the right decision.

By the way, that was very good coffee you made. Don't think I mentioned that.

Check your mailbox today.

Still gathering my thoughts about yesterday, maybe the most meaningful, for me, ever. No way I can thank you enough.

John

10:30 a.m.
John: It is amazing how much sunshine yellow tulips can bring into a day darkened by heavy clouds and steady rain. I went across the street to pick up my morning paper and was surprised to see the door hanging open and a package protruding from my mailbox. My mail doesn't usually arrive till afternoon. But it was all there. I had read your message earlier, so I knew you were the instigator. I've been smiling ever since. Thank you. I am basking In the glow.

Yesterday was like sunshine, too.

7:15 p.m., 4-7

Hi,

I suspect the box was delivered while we were talking. I had to make a snap decision, the day before, whether to allow the "Official U.S. Government Business" cachet to appear on the return (I declined, obviously) so it would have been easy for the package to just disappear. I was concerned about that. Maybe your post office knows better than to mess with a patron who flies the flag out front.

There was a corny, quickly-penned card inside the accompanying envelope. I had imagined that with 80 planter boxes on your deck you might well have several already out there with spring flowers.

Let me know how long they last. I can share them, vicariously, with you.

ILY

Sent Friday 4-8 8:15 a.m.

Hi,
One of my "agenda" items I never got to goes something like this: As lovely and memory-packed as is that marvelous home of yours, my heart aches at the thought of your being there *alone* so much of the time. This was the thing that really got to me when Geneve's e-mail mentioned it as a real problem for you a couple years ago, right after Cliff died.

So, I'm thinking, with the potential power of that fine computer of yours, if you ever need something different or new to absorb your mind, there's a whole world out there. Unless you can convince me this is an unnecessary path to walk, I'd like to think about giving you a short, simple "lesson," the next time I can get to your home, to show you how to search the world: art, music, anything you're interested in. It's not hard and you can do it, just with a few pointers to get you started. For example:

I just typed into Google the words "boutique art" and out jumped more than 3 million entries, easy to read (English only, if you wish) and just a click away.

What do you think?

Me

Sent 1 p.m., 4-8
I'm being a bit overwhelmed by the Pope's funeral today, primarily because of its international implications, more than one hundred "world leaders" in attendance, including some Muslims. One can certainly pray that the event will somehow

bring the world a little closer together, something my little group of writers is trying to promote, every day in every way. As I told you, Joan, it was Nine-Eleven that got me into this "temporary" job, I was so angry and I had to do *something* to get back into the fray.

Good Morning (12:30 a.m., 4-9),

If you look at the hour you'll be sure I am more than a little wacky. But you have sent 6 messages today, and I won't get up early enough to beat you to the computer.

The tulips began to open up today (Fri, 4-8). They were spectacular, deep blue black six sided stars down in the centers. Because it was sunny they looked even brighter than they did yesterday when I put them in water. Now they have closed up again and gone to sleep for a while. Smarter than I.

Yes, Sunday July 24th looks fine to me for our class mini-reunion. As far as I know now, the August dates are O.K. But I vote for July.

Of course, I would welcome any help to make me more computer literate. You probably would find it hard to believe that I have had a couple of computer classes through Bellevue Community College. The first one was before we even had a computer. Cliff, his office manager and I went together. Later, I took some by myself at the Bellevue library. When Cliff finally bought a computer for the office, he got one for home too. I couldn't get online during office hours because the two were somehow connected. I think I understood the old computer better than this one. I have never taken time to figure it out. I have already learned a couple of things from you and will be glad to learn more.

I've been thinking about your kite and sailplane flying. They seem to be connected. Do you feel that way about the two interests? I'm glad you've decided to stick to kites, now.

I got a DVD of Finding Neverland tonight. That is what kept me up so late. It was good but I am tired now.

Sent about 7:30 a.m., Sat., 9 Apr
What a lovely note to wake up to! You are so neat. Guess I haven't yet mentioned that I build and fly radio-controlled model airplanes, both wheeled and float planes. So, yes, there's a connection. Maybe I'm just "airy."

Sent 4:30 p.m., Sat 4-9 "Various"
Hello, again.

I'm sitting here, about 4 p.m. with a beautiful day going on outside, admittedly feeling a bit sorry for myself. I felt great yesterday, today kind of draggy. The doc warned me this chemo can be that way. Mostly, though, I'm daydreaming about walking with you in one of your lovely parks (I think I passed at least two on my way back Wednesday) with the Sunshine (that word, again) glinting through those marvelous old trees.

And—thinking about that brief phone conversation earlier today. Dear Lady, you have unwittingly added another item to my Agenda. I had to ask you to repeat your word "subversive," one I rarely use. After looking it up, for the first time ever, probably, I'm sure I know what you had in mind. My 15-man U.S. Marine guard contingent at our embassy in Moscow referred to me (out of range, of course) as "Sneaky Pete," understanding as they did my control over the comings and goings of all the spooks in the building. And today, this "sneaky" bit can be a worrisome thing and you just happen to be about the only person on this planet with whom I can talk about my present "temporary" job. A couple of cups of coffee with you should help, some day.

I'm worried about my birds. The swallows I mentioned many days ago only returned again today and the chickadees have shown no interest in their box of last year. Just another reminder that nobody outfoxes Mother Nature.

Well, enough. Tomorrow is Sunday, so go to bed earlier tonight! Your fine voice will be needed, well rested.

ILY

12:15 a.m., 4-10
John, I'm sorry you are feeling a little beat up. You had an energetic week with your office staff short-handed and all the efforts to put together the mini-reunion. Take care.

About definitions. Right after I said that, I knew it would be disturbing to you. First I grabbed a thesaurus to check for synonyms, then a dictionary to see what it said. My American Heritage Dictionary's second definition says "To undermine the character, morals or allegiance of." That is using the word Subvert. Subversive is intended or serving to undermine or overthrow, such as an established government. I wish I hadn't used it, I meant to be gently teasing.

Tonight I went out to a dinner party at the home of a friend who lives on Evergreen Point. She is a widow, too. She had two couples who are people I have known for a long time, but don't see often. It was a nice evening, four gals and two guys. I got home at about 10:30, but here I am at 11:30 because I hoped to find a message waiting for me. Now I can sleep.

4-10 Sunday, 7:30 a.m.
Good Morning,

That's the problem with the telephone and my crummy hearing. If I had seen your brown eyes sparkling, I'd have known you were teasing. But the Agenda item still remains to be addressed. Thanks, too, for sharing your evening. I'm glad you have friends like that.

Sent 8 p.m. 4-10
Hi,

Have I asked you?
What's your favorite ice cream? What do you like to go with it?

Did you know we have exactly the same dictionaries, I checked "subversive," even before you did!!

Sleep well, Dear Lady.

Sent 10:30 p.m., Sunday evening
Hi, John,

You need to know, if I haven't already told you, that Tuesday, I am having my two table bridge group here for lunch and the game. They arrive at 10:30 A.M. and hang around till about three.

It amazes me that you use the same dictionary as I. I keep thinking we are on the same page about many things. How about that?

This afternoon I went to the Pops Symphony. Usually the Seattle Symphony plays, but today it was the Tommy Dorsey Orchestra. Not my favorite from that era, brassy and loud, but full of nostalgia and music from our teen years. Nice to know the words that went with the music.

The tulips are still so fresh that I may be able to use some of them on my lunch table Tuesday. I am enjoying them every day. As for favorite ice cream, that could be a long dissertation. Are you curious?

Your favorite tease,

Sent morning 4-11
Hi,
Thanks for the reminder. I won't try to call Tuesday, you concentrate on your guests. I'll feel really "involved" if the tulips help with your plans. Have a great time with your friends.

Sent 3:20 p.m., 4-11
Subject: Names
Memory lane again. If I recall this, you surely must. First day of class (2nd, 3rd grade), new school year, new teacher. She reads off the names of her new students. She pronounces yours Joan (rhymes w/ loan). You correct her, loudly: "No, it's Jo-Ann!" She mumbles something about "usual" spellings. I'm sure I heard that happen at least twice maybe three times.

I really like the name the way you pronounce it, I suppose mainly because it's yours.

You can see where this is going? Diminutives (aka "affectionates") are tricky. For example, I've never liked Johnny, and few have tried it once they see that. I'm wondering in your case about Sunshine, which seems to fit so well (because it's so radiant in you), but I'd never consider it if others, especially Cliff, ever used it, and of course if it doesn't work for you. I think it's because, despite all the aches you've dealt with over your whole life, you're still, remarkably, a very sunshiny (can I say that?) person.

Well, that's my grand thinking for today. Afraid it'll have to do.

Me

Evening 4-11, before 8 p.m.
John, I am taking a break from my lunch preparations. I need it. Just set the table with tulips which look great. I thought maybe you would get this message before you turn in tonight. I am always writing at night owl hours it seems.

No one has ever called me Sunshine. Whatever special name you want for me is fine. I think I need all the sunshine I can get. I have always liked my name as long as it is pronounced Jo Ann. It never was a problem in school after I got those early teachers trained. Everyone in Sumner knew I was Jo*an. But it became a big problem as an adult. Whenever I used a name tag, I got called Joan, rhymes with loan. People argued about it with me. I did finally begin to put a star or a hyphen between the Jo and an. At least people notice and ask. It must have been a fashion when I was named. I have met other women in the same age bracket with the same problem. I think Joan is the feminine of John. My "stepmother" once sent me a birthday card which said it meant "Gift of God." That has always pleased me, and I think perhaps that covers your name too. Makes sense to me. No way are you a "Johnny."

Back to work. Good Night.

Sent 9 p.m. 4-11
Thanks for that, it makes perfect sense, as you always do. My mom told me I was named for John the Apostle, but I'll check on its meaning, never have, you're probably right. I know the two names are the same, i.e., masculine/feminine, although with some spelling variants. Some of those early languages had few or no vowels, so pronunciation was important to show differences.

Please don't overwork; enjoy your friends tomorrow. Your note ensures me a good night's rest. Thank you.

By the way, when you go to these after-dark events—theater, musicals, etc.,—are you ever alone, or always with someone? I might worry about that.

Sent 5:40 p.m., 4-12
Hi,

Well, I'm trying to telepathize (?) some extra energy your way, right now, knowing the clean-up is underway. I'm sure it was fun.

I'm going fishing Thursday or Friday, Central Washington, will meet a friend over there Saturday morning, assuming the chemo tomorrow is as benign as last week's (the one-week anniversary of our 2nd-ever "date"!). So I'll use the cell Thursday afternoon, evening or Friday, depending on how things go.

Don't wait around for my call, I'll find you eventually. Will you be home Fri evening?

Me

Sent 7:21 p.m., 4-12
I wish you had been hiding in a corner to hear the accolades for my tulips. Of course, my stunning arrangement had something to do with it, but I kid you not they were a huge success and made me secretly happy because of the source. The bunches that opened first fell apart today, but there was one bunch which had bigger blooms, longer stems and were yellow on the outside with an orangey interior. That's what I used for today. I have had over a week of pleasure from all those flowers and I will remember.

My friends arrived at 10:30 and four of the eight stayed till 4:30 playing bridge. Then I cleaned up. I need the extra energy you are trying to send. Try harder, I am really tired. I didn't sleep much last night.

In response to your concern over my after hour events. I usually go to the theater etc. with married couples who are long time friends. We have season tickets and plan for dinners in restaurants before, etc. Sometimes I go alone at night to dinner at the homes of friends, or meet friends in restaurants. I go to Bellevue Arts Museum parties alone, usually, and there will be more of those coming along soon because the Museum is finally opening again on June 18. Last Summer I went to dinner with a rather glamorous widowed woman friend. I had driven the convertible top down and planned to go home the same way. She made me put the top up. It was a beautiful summer night, but I did it. I think I've learned that lesson, but if you want to worry, you can.

Remember that I leave for choir practice at 7:15 on Thursday night, don't get home till around 9:30. So far, I have no Friday plans but it is my son's 47th birthday. Most likely he and his girlfriend will be celebrating with friends, but there is a chance that it could become a family thing Friday evening. Hope the fishing is good. And I hope the chemo is gentle. I pray for it every night . . . gentle and thorough.

Sent 8 p.m., 4-12
Oh, my. I'm sure the *party* was fun, not the clean-up. Sorry about that.

10 p.m., 4-12
The evil genius in me nearly came out this morning (5th grade Mrs. Cook knew about this trait, remind me to tell you sometime) as I considered urging you to hint to your bridge buddies that a "secret admirer" provided the flowers. Just a little mystery to add to the fun, but then I decided you'd do it anyway if you were in the mood for such. Did you take pictures of your arrangement? I'm sure you're very good at it and I'd love to watch sometime.

Sent 8:30 a.m., 4-13
Subject: Edits
Good morning, sure hope you're rested.

"Evil genius" was a bad choice. I was wracking my lousy memory for "impishness," which would have fit much better. In my defense, I sometimes have to compose these notes rapidly, usually a deadline coming up, either mine or one of the team's. But that's not much excuse for one in the writing/ editing business.

Anent your glamorous friend's view of after-dark top-down driving, I'm afraid I'm on her side. But my partial solution says that the next time you're out on a soft summer evening, after nightfall and top down, I'm sitting there beside you. You can be certain I'm developing an idea that could make this happen.

And, while we're working with words, "stunning arrangement" suits *you* as well as anything you do with flowers, at least that's my take on it.

Love you.

Reply 11 a.m., 4-13
Dear Evil Genius.

You make me laugh. That term didn't seem to fit and I was very curious to hear the end of the story. I still am.

You make me smile, too. I like your "partial solution" for the summer evening. I like having someone who says things that make me feel good. Thank you.

Evening 4-13, From Hitchcock's *Bible Names Dictionary*:

Joanna, grace or gift of the Lord

John, the grace or mercy of the Lord

These names look pretty close to me. Chemo went well. Gotta run.

Sent 2:30 p.m., 4-17
Hi,

I had wanted to send you a short note last night before bed but I was pretty tired and a little beat up, right and left calf both seized up from too much desert hiking between the lake and the parking area, after zero trips to the workout room for two months. And my computer at home has some glitches because of the office connection. It's okay for personal use, but Uncle really owns it so I have to be discreet.

Glad we connected yesterday afternoon, I liked that.

I usually have my lap-top with me in the motor home—desert or wherever I am—and I drafted this Thursday night, just an hour or so after the phone call from the phone booth.

Hey, Dear Lady, I really must apologize for part of that phone call from the desert phone booth, it must have seemed totally bizarre to you. I don't know what it is about phones with you at the other end, partly because I don't hear everything you say, and I'm kind of jelly-legged in your presence anyway, as you know by now. Maybe I should stick to e-mails.

Next time I can get away from this job for a full day, I'll have the *whole* day, and be with you as much or as little as you're up for. But I am serious about doing some fun-projects together, if that would help you out. If we can work in dinner and a top-down drive, fine, but helping you with "stuff" around the house seems like the most important. I would really enjoy that.

In the meantime, I'm learning that you're pleasantly busy with lots of good works and good friends. Whenever I can fit in, I'm pleased and proud.

But you still need to tell me your favorite ice cream, or maybe you don't even like the stuff! I do, sometimes, but it's not a passion, by any means. And then there are the faith stories of both of us, that we must cover some day and I want to learn a lot more about your interest in wine, and—. So a lot of ground to cover, still—

Now I'm thinking, before this friendship goes much further, you should go down to the Mercer Island courthouse and get a friendship contract, with a waiver built-in for you, so you can ditch this guy whenever he goes too far off the trail while on the phone.

Yr aging, sometimes dippy, friend

Sent 4:10 p.m., 4-17

Prowling through our '46 high school annual I find one pic of you, in the "juniors" page, with your classmates, wearing a very smart checkered skirt and jacket. Prettiest girl on the page, easily. And guess what?! You wrote a *whole page* in my annual!! Now that's treasure.

Rec'd 10 p.m., sent 5 p.m.

Thanks for warming my heart with that song. I listened to it over and over again. I do believe in angels. We need to share some of those experiences which made us believe.

As for ice cream, I switch favorites from time to time. Currently I am into Dreyers Light Carmel Delight. For many years I have stayed with the lower fat or fat free ice creams, probably never as tasty as the real thing. Of course, I do have moments when I get the yummy full fat treat when somebody else serves it, or I buy an ice cream cone. I can think of several kinds I have favored, among them Mocha Almond Fudge and Butter Brickle. Maybe I just like variety. Too bad I couldn't give you one definite. This must be more than you ever wanted to know.

For the past many minutes . . . more like a half an hour I have been unable to type anything. The computer was stuck. I hate that. I finally turned it off and started over.

You know I am flying to Oakland on Friday morning, renting a car and driving to the Sonoma valley for the Dry Creek Wineries Passport Weekend. Sonoma should be lush and lovely now. I'm looking forward to the scenery as much as to the wine. I have been Co-chairman of the Women's University Club wine committee, I know two couples who own wineries, Cliff and I ran a social wine tasting group for a couple of years. It was made up of about forty friends who held tastings in each others' homes each month. I really am not an expert, but because of Cliff's intense interest have been exposed to a lot of information

I am keeping a mental list of jobs that need to be done around here. By July there may be many more or maybe just different ones. Today as Libby was leaving, she discovered that the gutter over the garage was falling off. She did get up and nail it on, but who knows, it may need to be replaced. It's always something.

E-mail is a nice connection. I'm glad I have it. I find I check often these days because of you.

Sent 1:30 p.m., 4-18
Jo-Ann (love it!)

Whenever your computer locks up like that, don't wait. Just go through the shut-down sequence, carefully, and ask for a re-start. That very often will fix things.

Ice cream: Reminds of when I ate way too much good stuff and ballooned to 194, while I was in Moscow. I was number two in the station there, had a full-time job for the embassy, and worked for the Agency the other eight hours !! So my exercise consisted of running up and down stairs between my 5th floor apartment and my 9th floor office. Some deal, but probably the most challenging and rewarding of all my posts. Naturally, I can talk about that until everyone is sound asleep.

I'm excited about your "wine trip," and would like to know a little more, before you go. Hope we can connect.

As they say in Russian, "Po-KA," (a kind of affectionate 'until then'). John

Tue a.m. phonecon, 4-19

John's note to himself: A lovely conversation. Talked about choir previous Sunday, wine trip mostly, she had great interest in your two-job tour in Moscow. She's leaving Friday afternoon with Barbara and her two daughters, it's an arranged tour at that end, they'll come back Mon evening, probably late. This is something she and Cliff used to do often, he was always searching out good wines that didn't cost very much, as she put it. She's totally welcoming to her kitchen table any time you can make it. When you rang off with the overlapping good-byes, you said your final good-bye and then "love you." Her "Bye" following that was soft, smooth, melting, not at all cautious. Could this be happening?
Following above phonecon:
Hi,

Back in early March you said you like to listen to "smooth jazz." I just got a promo CD in the mail from 98.9, says on the label "Smooth Jazz, KWJZ." They're offering a drawing for a vacation to "Four Seasons Resort Maui." Want to go??!!

Seriously, if I take the time to listen to this will I be hearing what you're talking about? My education in this realm has a *long* way to go.

Before opening my e-mail Inbox this morning:

The two-by-four came down on the old mule's skull after a couple of hours: "Could *she* have—?" Of course, she did!

So, thank you, Jo-ANN.

Hi,

My pastor-son Mike has sent me several of his sermons on CDs but I can't play them on the DVD player in my pad. I have just one (part Uncle's) desk-top computer and it doesn't work well for just listening. So now I'm motivated to finally get one of those little things that works in your car off the cigar lighter. I like listening while driving better than at-home, anyway.

Great move, Dear Lady, I really appreciate it. Now I'll find out if you answered my silly response.

4-19, 11:36 p.m.
Re: Jazz

Good morning John,

Here I am again after 11:00 P.M. I just got home from dinner and bridge at a friend's house. It was ladies only, but the hostess is 46 and has a 4 year old who likes to be among the guests. He is a super bright red-headed little boy who reads almost anything and runs around like crazy. One of the other women demands constant attention and ended up spilling a glass of red wine on my white jacket. Later she abruptly stood up from the dinner table and said she had to go home and was gone. The hostess was horrified. This was only a party of four. Any way, not the best of evenings, and I was glad to find a cheerful note from you to change my mood before I go to sleep.

Listen to that smooth jazz and see how you like it. I'm not crazy about Dixieland, but mellow smooth jazz with interesting instrumentals sounds good to me.

Hawaii is my favorite place. I'd go anytime. I haven't made it for the past year and a half which is unusual. I miss it. Have you been there? The minute I get off the plane I feel myself go Ahhhhh, and my whole body relaxes. But I love Honolulu best, because there is a big variety of things to do and special out of the way places that I am fond of.

One more thing tonight. Yesterday I searched through our "45" and "46" HS annuals. There was a note from you to me, in the 45 edition. You told me that you always did think that I was a pretty swell kid. And I wrote you a whole page? I hope I said nice things. Back then we'd only known each other for 10 years, give or take a few months. Now it has been 70. Seems unreal.

Your very long time friend,

Jo*an

Sent 1:45 p.m. 4-20
Hmmm, such a coy kid. I guess it really was you who engineered that CD-in-my-mailbox. When I first saw it, that was the last thing in my mind but then after awhile: too coincidental.

I dunno about ladies like that. I feel bad for you and your dress, and you must have had excellent self-control.

44

Hey, fair's fair. Next time at your breakfast table we'll share annuals. You need to know that I had reserved three pages for you in the '46 edition (what does that say?) and you were gracious enough to fill one.

I'll say more about Hawaii when I have more time (always a problem). I love it too, haven't been there for too long, used to go mostly to Maui for the snorkeling.

2 p.m., 4-20
Dear music lover,

Honestly, I had nothing to do with that C.D. It *is* a coincidence. No kidding. I had to go to a meeting in Bellevue today . . . Bellevue Arts Museum stuff . . . I got in the convertible, put the top down, turned on FM radio to 98.9 and listened to smooth jazz on the way over and back. Wish you had been there to share the breezes and the sound.

7:30 p.m., 4-21
Dear Tease,

Well, now that we have that little mystery cleared up—

I should probably scold you for offering such a delectable, beyond-reach image: Jo-an, soft jazz and the top down. Maybe *you* have an impish streak, too. Yes, to be a mouse in your pocket these next few days is to die for. So enjoy a bit for me, too! Be safe, above all else. I'll pray for that, and more, for sure.
Yr ol' buddy

CHAPTER 6

Off to Sonoma Country

Sent 4-21 (Thur) 2:40 p.m.
Yes, something *is* missing here. My cousin Kitty, since losing her husband, always lets me know her airline itinerary whenever she travels, "just in case." I'm wondering if you'd care to join this group of one, for similar reasons??

Sent 5:30 p.m., 4-21
Alaska Airline 326 Depart Seatac 10:15 am Fri, April 22 Arrive Oakland 12:17 pm

Alaska Airline 459 Depart Oakland 8:31 pm Mon, April 25 Arrive Seatac 10:25 pm

Staying at Geyersville Inn. (707) 857-4343

You make me feel protected. Libby will have this info, too. At our ages, who knows what may happen? If California has a big earthquake while I am down there you know where I am supposed to be.

I liked the pictures you sent. I don't know how to make them small enough to see in one view. I have to scroll and I want to print them as soon as I get my new ink cartridge. I feel so dumb about computers but you seem to have easy answers that help.

Thanks for the sweet Bon Voyage words. I am on super overload today with too many meetings and obligations. I need to escape from the pressures. I will connect on Tuesday. Thanks for adding interest and a special friendship to my life.

After Joan's return from Sonoma:

Sent 4-25, 3 p.m.
Subject: Bedtime Reading

Hi, weary traveler, and welcome back!

I'm taking a chance, here, knowing you'll be getting home quite late and quite tired and that e-mail is probably the furthest thing from your mind. In case you see this for the first time in broad daylight you'll know why they say timing isn't always everything, but it can help!

Po-KA.

While you were away
Your world was not the same.
That warming smile was missed by some
A voice of hope not there.
The grieving mom was pleased to wait
'Til your return to care.
Others noticed just as well,
Your circle slight less round.
Colleagues seeking steady wisdom,
Mom's eager ear not found.

But God's creation beckoned you,
As no doubt it would.
Time to be with loved ones,
Precious ones who could
Help you reflect, remember
Joyous times before
God's mysterious ways
Denied your evermore.

Everyone who knew
Your walking with your God
Understood your way-ness,
Your call to be abroad.
And God is pleased
You serve Him well,
He knows your every need.
You've seen His mighty hand for long,
In fruit and vine and seed.

So now you're home, in good repose,
Memories fresh to savor.
Your world awaits tomorrow
When you will give it favor.
So in this note's a virtual hug,
A 'Welcome Home' for you.
With wishes for the deepest sleep
And dreams of marvel, too.
Dreams in which your God smiles down
On all the things you do
For others as your minds entwine,
To help them turn anew.

So while you were away
Your world was not the same.
But now God's arms are holding you,
To sigh again His name.
He loves us all with all His might
But with a special place
For one like you who knows
How marvel we His grace.

So sleep and dream
My special friend,
Tomorrow's not yet here.
For joy awaits with all her love
Someone like you, so dear.
—

Sent about 11 a.m. 4-26
John,
Last night I slept very well after your "bedtime reading." I did check my e-mail first, and was very impressed by your lovely poem. I felt some of those feelings about God as I flew through the night sky. I prayed thanks for the beauty of His world, and I prayed for you. My traveling companions were seated three across on the seats in front of me. I had the window seat behind and strangers next to me, so I spent most of my time in thought.

The Sonoma Valley is lush and a treasure of God's creation. I love it. The "Passport Weekend" is really an orgy of food and wine. There are musicians at almost every winery, and, of course, the unique feeling of each place. The buildings, the gardens, the views, the atmosphere and presentation all add to the ambiance. Among lots of other things we ate wild boar, calamari, very thin slices of raw salmon marinated in zinfandel. There were oysters on the half shell (I don't eat those) and lots of fabulous chocolate goodies to go with the red wines. You start at 11:00 am and go until 4:30 pm if you can hold up that long. We did. You get tastes of the chosen wines with the foods . . . not glasses full. About six wines are offered at each winery. It takes a while to drive on to the next place and most places you have to walk a ways from the parking place. Some had shuttles. No one seems to get drunk. We hit five places the first day, six the second. There were 30 to choose from.

Yesterday we crossed over the mountains between the Sonoma and Napa Valleys and went to visit a friend of mine in the new winery that she, her husband and son are building. They are not open yet but have grown the grapes, built a beautiful home and the first wine is in barrels and will be sold next year, I think. Her husband has a personal wine cellar of twenty thousand bottles of wine collected over the years, all kept in controlled environment. We got to see it. Pretty amazing. We drank coke.

Nuff said. Too much, no doubt, but I think I'll keep this for my personal travelogue as well.

Your wandering friend,

Jo*an

Here, John inserts a note about Joan's uncanny knack for attracting unusually interesting friends. The winery is owned by Louis Kapscandi, a Hungarian by birth who escaped the Hungarian Revolution of 1957 and came to the United States. He had been an excellent soccer player in his native land and soon caught on with the Los Angeles Rams' professional football team as its place kicker! "The rest is history."

Sent Tue, 4-26, 12:25 p.m.
About those e-mail pictures, there should be one or more icons shown across the "Attachments" line, which is usually right under the "Subject" line in the upper left corner of the window. In this case I believe they're titled 'Lenice Lake 4-05' with a three-digit number following. Just left-click once on the icon and the photo should come up and just fill the screen. If that doesn't work, let me know and we'll try something else.

I'm anxious to spend a few minutes with you at your machine, while you run it, to get a better idea of what goes on with your particular system.

And it looks like noon-to-four, or any part of that frame, will work for me, May (*Friday*) 13th, for coffee and chat. I know that's getting into your busy time and maybe, even, you're superstitious! What do you think?

Sent 10:40 p.m., 4-26
Subject: Coffee and Chat

Friday, May 13 noon to four or somewhere in between, no superstition about the date. Libby's birthday is March 13. We have celebrated Friday birthdays. The calendar is marked.

So far I have managed one good print of your fishing buddy in Lake Lenice. I'll try for others later. I have to do tomorrow's meeting agenda now.

Sleep well.

Sent an hour after ½ hr phonecon afternoon 4-27

Hi,

Don't know what it is about your voice but it sure is uplifting, like about 10 feet off my tiny shop floor. So I went out and did some light weeding in my little bird sanctuary, to come down to earth. Thanks for giving up some very nice weather, out-of-doors, to talk.

PLEASE, don't overdo! I (we all) want you to stay healthy for a lot more years.

ILY

Sent 10 p.m., 4-27
Hey, my dear friend,

It was a pleasure to share some time with you. I felt like I did most of the talking. You ask a lot of questions about me. I would like to get more information on what has to be the very interesting life you chose for yourself. Mine is mundane in comparison. It works for me, but I really am interested in whatever things motivated you. I think catching up will take a long time, our seventy year friendship hasn't been long enough.

Happy day today, and tomorrow and more,

Jo! an

Sent about 10 a.m., 4-28
Hi,

Seems I grabbed the flu bug last night, kind of wiped out right now, sure it's temporary but I may not get to my keyboard much until this passes. Sorry. Think I'll try your cool, virtual hand on my hot forehead for awhile!

Sent 5:30 p.m., 4-28
John, I feel bad cuz you feel bad. I am sorry, and I keep thinking you don't need this on top of the chemo. I am not so sure my hands are cool, but I am sending cooling thoughts for your hot head and prayers that this will be over in a short time. God bless and make you well very soon. Rest well, take care and let me know how you are when you can.

Love,

Joan

Sent about noon 4-29
Subject: Word choices

Now, come on, Dear Lady, you can do better than that! *Mundane*? Look it up in our dictionary: worldly, yes; ordinary, no. I suspect that was your meaning.

I could name a dozen women, roughly our age, in my church whom I know well enough and who would envy without end your track record of (1) *applied* talent, (2) service, (3) positive impact on others, (4) taking care of yourself (emotionally and physically)—and I could go on.

The "news" I would have given you yesterday: About two hours' in the car cumulatively on 98.9, on Tuesday, and I really liked it, especially the first piece I happened on to which was a classical (I think) guitar and some other instruments doing something that reminded me immediately of Spanish dance and I think it was called "Madrid." I really ate that stuff up (Flamenco, etc.) during an R&R in Spain in the '60s. There was a former Rockette on the embassy staff in Tehran and she ran a dance class for clods like me, even got so I could do a respectable tango. Hard to believe, now.

My flu bug hit hard but only for about 24 hours, thanks plenty to your prayers. I'm still a little wobbly but definitely over it.

This probably is more than I need to write in one sitting but I'm always alone in this bachelor pad of mine and I just felt like it. So there! Love you.

Sent 1:30 p.m., 4-29
O.K., Dear Sir, I got out our dictionary and was surprised at what it said. It didn't mention ordinary. Then I opened two thesaurus (I don't know what is plural for that) and read the synonyms of mundane in both. One gave ordinary, everyday, commonplace etc., as first synonyms. The other gave worldly first. You are stretching my mind. One day you used anent. I had to look that up. Challenges are good but, I loved the things you said after the scolding.

I am glad you are better. I worried about you all morning as I led exercise, then went to Costco in Issaquah to get flowers and fruit for the Memorial Reception I am putting together for my friend. I was anxious to get home to see if you were feeling good enough to e-mail. Thank God, you were.

You listened to 98.9 and liked it. HOORAY! I listened while I drove this morning.

I am impressed that you learned to tango. That is a dance that I never really conquered, but I love to dance and have had lots of ballroom dance lessons. Have I told you that from age 48 to 56 I tap danced. I loved that too, but eventually the knees couldn't take it anymore. Still have the tap shoes though.

Stay better.

Sent 7:30 p.m., 4-29

Subj: You will never live this down

See, you make my case: Taking up tap dancing in middle age is NOT mundane!

Sleep well, Sunshine.

CHAPTER 7

Two People in Love!

John recalls that the last lines of this next entry were probably, for him, the most precious of the 200+ pages of e-mails that accumulated throughout their love-story exchange.

Next afternoon, 4-30, about 10 minutes on the phone. Joked around about "anent" and dancing. She still has the tap shoes and I asked her to see them. She did some gigs w/ another friend for Cliff's (50th?) birthday wearing stocking garters, at home. Teen Libby thought her mom had flipped and ran all over the neighborhood asking people to come watch. She said she can't make it for dinner Monday, has to help Libby fix her car. I told her it looked bleak for the 13th because of my work schedule. That was bad news for her, too, we definitely want to see each other soon. At the usual goodbyes: I: "Bye, love you." She: "I love you, too. Bye." *First time **ever** those words have passed her lips, en route to your ears!*

(And much later in their e-mail exchanges Joan writes to John: "I only spoke my heart, 'I love you too, John,' and our whole world changed almost instantly.")

Sent 6 a.m., 5-1
Good morning,

This is a very good thing you are doing today, Jo-Ann. I'm praying often that it will go just as you want it to. I think God's hands are going to be all over this.

Bless you.
Sent 6 p.m., 5-1

Subj: Le Danse

I'm still chuckling over your garter exposé. I guess Libby did get over it, eventually.

Thinking that Cliff must have been a very good dancer, for a couple of reasons. One, he had super motivation to do you justice and, two, a Marine combatant almost would have to be a good dancer: quick on the feet, nimble, purposeful (and fearless?). Am I close? Anyway, I can easily envy him all those ballroom experiences with you!

I suspect that tonight you are tired, relieved, and happy that you did what you did. As you should be.

You've earned good rest. Enjoy.

ILY

Sent 7:30 p.m., 5-1
I found the pictures. They are acceptable enough that I showed them in a photo display of Cliff's life at his memorial in my church. You will see them just to help you understand me in my goofier moments. He and I did have fun dancing. I am glad to know you made efforts along those lines, too.

I appreciate your thoughts and encouragement as I headed off to my commitment this morning. It was a long and exhausting day, but successful and fulfilling as well. It was nearly six when I got home. Ten thirty a.m. when I began setting up. I know I helped ease the pain of people I care about. That is what counts.

John, you affirm me. That is such a blessing. I can't express how much it means to me to know you care.

Love you,

"Jo-an," Hey, My siblings call me Jo. So did my college friends. Few people do that any more. I liked it when you used Sunshine. Whatever you choose is ok with me.

Sent 9:30 p.m., 5-1
I may get in the last word tonight!
I think Jo-ANN, just the way your folks gave it to you, is perfect; and I love it. "Sunshine" is in that "affectionate-diminutive" category and I'll use it occasionally, but only when the "feel" is right. You'll sense it, I hope. (That's the problem with words without faces, you have to guess a bit.)

I am so glad your day was successful. Many people were enriched by the little things you probably didn't even think about. That's just the way you are. If that's "affirming," so be it, but it's the truth.

'Night.

John forwarded his cousin Kitty's desert flowers photo with a note something like:

About 8 a.m., 5-2,
Good Morning, I've been fond of desert flowers for some time and knew of this 100 year event but this is the first photo evidence I've seen. Leave it to Kitty! ILY

Sent 2 p.m., 5-2

Thanks for the gorgeous desert flowers. They are spectacular. Have I told you that we used to spend a couple of weeks each winter in either Palm Springs or Palm Desert? For about six years we owned a town house in a country club there with another couple. It was supposed to be a business deal. We rented it out which made it difficult for us to use during the best times to be there. We finally got sick of that and sold it. We started going to the desert when we were in our forties and into tennis. We stayed at the Tennis Club in Palm Springs. Eventually, that was turned into time shares and the atmosphere changed, so we went other places. Geneve and I always got together when we were there, but I haven't been back for more than two years.

As you know Monday is my busy morning. When I got home I checked my e-mail and started writing this. Just now, up popped two new messages from you. One made me teary but comforted. As for the other, I think I will be home in time for us to talk. Be prepared.

List of things to take on 5-13: '46 annual, Agency award invite to Kitty, Osprey Kamchatka piece, maybe the Ressam story, map of Iran.

Incredible phonecon, about 1 hr, 5-2, 8 to 8:50 p.m. I kidded/chided her for saying the ILY2 words at the end of the call on Saturday and she said, "Well, I really do. Are you surprised?" She said it again at the end of the call ("I love you, too, John"). You could never have anticipated this and you need to be patient, because when *two* people love each other they want to spend all their time together and you can't give her that, not for awhile.

Topics: The reception yesterday was at the VFW hall, presided by a pastor who knew the family and came from California to preside. The grieving mother is a member of J's church, most of the 90 (invite only) attendees are believers. The twin who took his life is about 50. Step-father is in mid-80s, good friend of J's for many years, wife/mother is 78. The twins are/were *both* bi-polar so the family has had a lot of concern over the years. She worked on the reception from ten until cleanup at 5;30, then crashed at home.

She may send me some scripture to comment on, part of her prep for the bible study she does with other ladies each Monday, work on passages of relevance to the upcoming sermon each Sunday. I encouraged her to do so.

She'll make sandwiches for the 13th.

Sent 9:25 p.m., after phone call
Subj: Love

Hi, Sunshine,

58

This IS one of those times for that name.

I think I probably don't deserve you, but I'm not going to argue about it. Being in love with you for sixty-nine years is a very long time, maybe Guinness would be interested, but worth every minute. I don't think guys are supposed to "bask in the glow," as you talked about what the tulips did for you. Your expression of love for me does that, by a factor of light years.

Now we need to talk about where this goes, carefully.

In the meantime, I think I'll sleep better tonight than in years.

Thank you, Jo-an. I've said it before and can't much improve on it: You are *so* special.

John

Tue a.m., 5-3
Good Morning,

Here's an example of a Word attachment, just click on the paperclip icon or whatever you have near the top, probably just under the Subject line: Your bible study notes.

Hope you slept well, I surely did!! ILY

Written 7:30 5-3, read 1030

John, I got the Word attachment and read it all, it will really help me. This morning I am making a fast trip to Redmond to pick up my company quarterly tax reports. They were supposed to be mailed yesterday. I'll probably get fined. Thanks for showing me another new thing that can be done on the computer. Happy day.

Sent about noon 5-3
Pretty early for you to be doing e-mail. I don't want you being fined by the tax authorities *or* by the cops: What is a "fast" trip

to Redmond? Yours looks like a great study, some of Jesus' toughest teachings. Love you.

Sent 5 p.m., 5-3

Hi,
I'm sensing our friendship has been elevated a bit, so I'll be even more bold than previously, knowing your fly swatter is handy if you choose to use it.

I've been very curious for some time to see you with your hair "down," however that works. For example, in a longer-than-usual hug, the guy is disposed to run his fingers through her hair. I think we can both remember that, though it might be a challenge. With the 13th coming up, I'm hoping you'd be willing to think about this.

Imp

Sent 9:45 p.m., 5-3
Hey, I don't have a *right* to hear from you every day, but after more than 24 hours since last evening, and your "fast" trip to Redmond this morning, I'm just a tad concerned as I head for bed. I hope your jail cell was comfy but that they let you out in time to get home to turn into your own bed. Seriously, you okay? Love you.

Sent 9:44 p.m., 5-3
Subj: Laughter
JOHN, everything I just read made me laugh out loud. That is supposed to be really good for my health, so I am grateful. Last night, after our chat on the phone and while you were blissfully sleeping, I was in a state somewhere between sleep and wakefulness. I thought about you all night long. I looked at the clock about every hour, checking to see if I had slept. Then I went back into a mid-slumber state thinking about you till morning came. I felt remarkably good when I got up, but it caught up with me this evening. I sat down to watch TV while my dinner cooked

in the oven and didn't wake up till almost nine o'clock. I ate a very overcooked dinner and here I am.

I *will* let my hair down for you. In fact, I have wondered if you might ask me that. I must warn you though. My family have always said I look like a witch when I let my hair down. I do it on a regular basis once a year. Every Halloween for many years I have let my hair down, put on an all black outfit and a witch's hat and have worn it all day, No MATTER WHERE I HAVE BEEN. I have been on several airplanes that way, and a cruise ship. Last year I mingled with the children from the pre-school in my church as they partied in their cute non-witchy costumes. Not a very holy scene, but I had fun. No one complained. One year I was waiting in the John Wayne airport for Cliff to pick up a rental car. It is funny that most people carefully look the other way when they see a witch sitting there alone, but one man came walking close to me and said, "You remind me of my EX—wife!"

P.S. A longer than usual hug sounds good to me. You won't have to wait till Halloween, just ask.

I am sorry if I worried you about my quick journey to Redmond. I did make it fairly rapidly but stayed within the speed limit. No stops or shopping on the way there or back. No tickets, no accidents, just came home to do hours of paper work, bill paying etc. till I fell asleep. Now I'm off to bed. I love thinking about you, but tonight I'll hope for peaceful slumber.

Love you. Joan

Sent 2:30 p.m., 5-4
Let me warn you, Dear Lady, this sleep-deprivation thing might be contagious. I've been thinking about *you*, 24/7, for several months and it does make sleeping soundly a bit problematic. I thought it might be the chemo but finally faced up to the lovely truth.

I'm a bit surprised Cliff let you get away with actually thinking you look like a witch when your hair is down, although I imagine there was a lot of tongue in cheek involved. You'd be beautiful bald, in my eyes.

Come to think of it, the witch in Snow White was really a beautiful queen, wasn't she? She had to work hard to make herself witch-like. You'll have to convince me that's not a good parallel in this case.

I expect the "down" configuration for at least part of our time on the 13th. Fair enough?

Love you, extremely!

Sent 7:30 p.m, 5-4

Jo-an, I'm dazzled by your spontaneous and fun-loving antics, something I haven't seen much of over the years. I'm beginning to realize, thanks to you, what I've missed. It's a part of you I wouldn't have been able to guess, but I love you even more for it. Maybe it's not too late for a bit to rub off.

And just so you know, *no one* (absolutely, no one) has ever told me about *thinking* about me. Can you possibly imagine how that sounds to these tired old ears??

Yes, I think a longer-than-normal hug is called for, hair down of course.

Do sleep well, my Beauty. I'll try very hard to do the same, but no guarantees.

John

Sent 6:45 p.m., 5-4
JOHN, It is me again, about to have my singular dinner. In case I fall asleep in front of the TV, knowing that you turn in way before I do, I want you to know that you are ever in my thoughts and prayers. Maybe you have figured that out by now. You cannot

know that I am experiencing intense feelings that have been buried for a very long time. I am scared about what is happening to me. Who could ever believe that this could happen at 75. Sleep well my love, Joan

John sends this e-mail to Joan just after returning from their May class luncheon

Sent about 4 p.m., 5-5
My most precious one,

Goodness, it was wonderful to see you there, among all our old friends.
I'm a little scared, too. When you asked me if I was surprised you used the "ILY2" words I was so flabbergasted I don't think I ever answered your question. I've always hoped you'd *like* me enough to allow a friendship that works but never in my wildest imagination could I have foreseen what's happened to us recently. Yes, we're both 75 but our spirits, I think, have become a whole lot younger. "Scared" is really fear of the unknown, there's no "map" for this but I think we can make it work. I need to finish my story and now I think I'd like to know about your "buried intense feelings" if you're willing to share—and *only* that much. So we have a lot to talk about on the 13th and we both need to pray that nothing happens to mess up the plan.

I'm crazy about you, Joan. Thank you so much for coming today.
John

Sent about 3:30 p.m., 5-5

Dear Best Friend,
Tonight is Choir practice again. I have had a two week reprieve from practice because of the Sonoma trip, and last week we didn't sing on Sunday so no rehearsal. You'll no doubt be tucked in by the time I get home. Sweet dreams.

Love You, Joan

Subj: I'm sorry
My Most Precious Person,

Forgive me, Joan, for speaking too quickly. I think your suppressed feelings are probably none of my business until and unless you want to say otherwise. I'm truly sorry.

I'm sitting here realizing I'm tired, both physically (little sleep last night) and emotionally, so I have a glass of red wine on my computer desk. Guess what, it's out of a *box*, Franzia "Merlot." I'm sure you've never ever tried such but I got used to it on heavy-equipment helo fishing trips. Guys who fish that way can afford bottled wine but they prefer boxes 'cause they don't break. These days, I have no excuses. And it's no more likely to leave a headache than good wine is, I've found.

As I said the last time we were together, I have always thought of you as my Goddess, on a pedestal above everything beautiful I can imagine. It's a Greek idea, of course, and they were very good romantics. I've felt that way about you for so long it's hard to remember when the idea first came to me but whenever that was it has never left. And I really mean that.

John

Sent 8:40 p.m., 5-6
Anything is acceptable when you are worn out. Remember, you still are undergoing treatment! I forgive you, but if you hang out with me you will undoubtedly keep a small supply of something a *little* more elegant. I do go for cheap but tastes good. My local newspaper's wine writer recently did a column on some reasonably good boxed wines.

I hold you in my heart with love, thankful that you are part of my life.

Joan

Sent 10 a.m., 5-7
Sweetheart,
As we might say in diplo-speak, we now have a week to go for our second round of talks. Those sandwiches might go well with some of your cheap-but-good *vin*. Have I told you that since Olympia passed that night-in-jail-no-questions-asked law (breathalyzer results?) I've refused to drive even after one beer? But I'm thinking that with a little food and a couple of hours before driving—and with you as primary motivation—I could make an exception! Hmmm.

Dreamed about you early this morning, first time since my Vienna Vision. Nothing quite so vivid this time, and different. We were *together*, much younger of course, on a ski vacation at a place that had no roads to it, only a wooded airstrip (from my B.C. wilderness fly-ins, no doubt—met Dick Cheney on one of these, by the way, but I digress). We had had a wonderful day, you were laughing and flashing that incredible smile of yours, and then, bingo, we are separated, you're lost in the crowd, sun is going down, we have no overnight reservations and *must* make the last bush plane out before dark, and I'm praying *Dear God, don't let me lose her!* And I woke up, thankfully. My, oh, my.

Sent 12:30 p.m., 5-7
My! *Goddess,* yet. I love it. I read that paragraph and laughed out loud to think you would call me that. You have a way with words that obviously is a delight to me. I am still smiling.

Now I am on my way to pick up Libby. She decided we should go today for Impatiens for the shady spots on my deck. She will buy them and help me prepare the pots and boxes that hold them. That is my Mother's Day gift from her. Besides that we will be going to the Bellevue Botanical Gardens tomorrow afternoon with Barbara and her daughters for a special program that includes tea and music. Then the "girls" will prepare our dinner. Sounds good.

Your two dreams were similar except that in the one last night we started out together. I remember the first one, but I don't have it. I think it was on my old computer.

Later love,

Just plain me

Sent noon, 5-8
John, I was so glad you called this morning. It really brought me joy. I'm off to all my Mother's day activities. Won't get home till after dinner tonight. I just wanted to tell you again, I love you.

Joan

Sent 5:30 p.m., 5-8
Sunday evening. I can't believe I could phone you *twice* this morning and forget to say what I mainly called about: Have a beautiful Mother's Day, and it sounds like you will.

I did a word search of my now-55-page collection of "notes" between us, since February (!) and can find "Goddess" only once, so you are forgiven for not remembering it from earlier on. But I'm pretty sure I spoke of it, several times. Anyway, it's a beautiful picture, for me anyway, and we can review it in a few days, I hope.

"Plain" you?? Come on, Jo-an. We're talking *royalty* here!

More tomorrow. I love you, too, never doubt it.

Sent 8 p.m., 5-8
Hi,
The lectern readings today included your passage from Acts about the visible ascension and I surely thought about you, again, at that moment. Then in the sermon we were reminded that all people are built (wired) by God for *relationships*, relationships of love with each other and with Him. I like that

very much, the idea may explain how we have come to love each other as we do.

Sleep well, tonight, by Most Precious Person. My, how I do love you!

John

Sent 9:30 p.m., 5-8
Just got home from a very full day. It was wonderful. Our church service was also built around the ascension story, but our childless woman pastor preached a Mother's Day sermon using the love and sharing of women for their children and families as example of the spreading of God's love. It was really upbeat. During our "Joys and Concerns" prayer time, a beautiful black woman from South Africa, who joined our congregation quite a few months ago when she first came here, spoke of her joy in being a mother. She was pregnant when she came, not married and the congregation had taken her under its wing. When her son was born a couple of months ago, a woman who sings in the choir and her husband, (white) took on the role of surrogate grandparents. That baby gets shown around at coffee time after the service often. Everyone left feeling good.

We had a wonderful guided tour of the Bellevue Botanical Gardens. I will be helping to organize the display of art for the Patron's Party which precedes the Bellevue Arts and Crafts Fair in late July. The Fair helps fund the Bellevue Arts Museum which you must know by now I am involved in. The Party will be held at the Botanical Gardens, so I was checking it out for that, too. The weather was perfect for enjoying the beautiful plantings in this lovely park. When we left there we went to my two nieces' house and played scrabble, ate dinner and finally I came home. It was a good day but I thought of you often and wished you could have been with me.

Tomorrow is busy Monday, so I'll be gone early and not home till well after one.

I was happy to get your messages when I got home tonight. I always am.

Love you, Joan

Sent 9:15 a.m., 5-9
Hi, Interesting that as I was getting dressed this morning, and before reading your lovely account of your Mom's day, I was thinking about how frustrated I'm becoming by my limited opportunities to "share your world." We have so many likes in common—most of the cultural world, I suspect, although I'm a lout about art—but concerts, plays, readings, exhibits, gardens, yes, wine tastings, I love all this stuff and am longing to get back to it. Sometimes I think I should quit this job, as much a commitment it is, and see if someone else couldn't step up. But there's a vicarious awakening going on in these old bones, Joan, thanks, blessedly, to you!

ILY. John

Sent 5:30 p.m., 5-9
You always say the right thing. No wonder I love you. When I finished my message last night, I thought it might be boring to you. You made me feel good about it as you do about everything. Another thing that gets me is your "So there." I can hear you saying that in grade school! Do you remember that? We were walking across the street from the Berryland and you said to me "I know how to make babies!" Then you sort of swished your bottom at me and said, "So there!" It reminds of how long our friendship has endured.

ILY2

Sent 7:30 a.m., 5-10
Guess what? By the time you see this, I may even have a follow-up report. So why bother to write now? Because any "connection" I can make with you is joy to my heart, Dear Lady, so there!!

I honestly don't remember that Berryland thing but it doesn't surprise me. Anything to get your attention. My mom had told me the birds and bees story some time when I was in kindergarten, so I'm guessing my bottom-swishing act happened in first grade.

Love you. John

Hey, You!

Do you know that you could write about your new power toothbrush, or about how you do your hair "up" like that, or anything else, and it would *never* be 'boring' to me. I love every word and I've said that before. In fact I'd like you to take me through the Botanical Gardens some time. I love those places.

Gotta scoot, sorry. Love you *so* much!! John

5 p.m., 5-10
Oh, the telephone!

My life would be so much simpler (not to mention joyful) if I had just married you in 1951!

Height of presumption? Probably.

One of my team couldn't make it to work today, so I'm afraid Friday won't work. Thursday evening might be okay if you're willing to have me come, say as late as 8 p.m. and then kick me out whenever This is a bit bold, Joan, so don't feel shy about telling me to "cool it, Buster!"

Stay tuned. ILY

After our phonecon:
Thank you for "inviting" me. How dumb of me to forget about choir practice, the thought of being with you destroys all other senses!

Sent 9 p.m., 5-10: By the way, which car are you likely to drive to choir practice, black or tan?

Her justifiably impatient response:

The convertible is SILVER. It matches my hair, but I will probably drive the black one to choir practice. I will leave my house at about 7:15, will definitely be back by 9:30, maybe sooner.

"Moses" made me laugh. I need a lot of that in my life. You add some, but you also add a lot of consternation . . . most of which are things over which you have no control because of your demanding work schedule. My love for you crept up on me. I know it is there to stay, but it is not easy because I am so impatient to be with you.
In the meantime JOHN, I loved the card and especially your personalization of it. I think I will put it under my pillow and dream on it.

Many hugs, I love you

Joan

Sent 3 p.m., 5-11
Boy, did I step in that one! Of course it's silver and of course it matches your hair, and of course I knew that. How long since you gave me that spin around the block from the I-Hop in your Silver Bullet, from which I am still spinning?! Brain lock, damaged goods, all of the above.

Last chemo this morning. Feeling pretty good. I have coveted your prayers, my precious one. Thank you, so much. John

FROM: **Joan**
To: John
Sent: Wednesday, May 11, 2005 7:40 PM
Subject: I am confused

It has been a long and satisfying day for me. I did a lot of driving with four people as passengers in my car. The trip to Whidbey and the sculptor's studio was truly fulfilling for lovers of art.

When I came home after over eight hours of travel, I came almost immediately to my computer hoping for your words. What I received was a nearly complete history of our computer connection over the past months. How did you do that? I got your personal thoughts and comments about my reactions to what you said, and yours to mine. In a way, it was like reading your personal diary. I read it all. It took well over an hour. It is like a love story, looked at from both sides. Maybe we could publish it with a bit of polishing. I think what I really want to know is why you did that?

I have cooked my dinner, but I came back down here to write this before I eat, because I want you to have this before you turn in. I need a response. And of course, I want to know about tomorrow night. You are right that people who love each other want to be together. We have had little of that.

Joan

Sent 7:48
Had my dinner. Hope you got my response back again.

Despite my confusion I still feel the same way about you and want to see you tomorrow night.

P.S. I want to be kissed.

Sent 8 p.m., 5-11
Quickly. Yes, I've managed a shift change so I can come over after your choir practice. Oodles of kisses (not yet discussed, have we?)
ILY, John

PS. Just read your latest. I am embarrassed beyond words, it was a terrible mistake, I have no idea how it happened. Clearly some of those notes were only for my later recollection. I can be pretty hard on myself and I needed to try to sense how you were responding, I was sometimes terrified I would put you off, hurt you, or some other terrible thing. And it is so important to me that I never misread you. It is unbelievably sweet of you to put such a positive spin on what you read. Can we talk about this???

Sent 8:30 5-11

Joan,

I was so shaken by what you just wrote that I zapped it before I could add it to my electronic diary, of which you now know all. Would you mind re-sending it? It's such a remarkably forgiving piece, and so like you.

I feel hopelessly in your power, Dear Lady. I don't deserve you and yet you persist on putting up with me! What an incredible blessing.

You are beautifully innocent, Joan. I am not. I've been in the spook business for so long I have to work at shedding the old habits. You will teach me more about that and I long to have it happen.

Please sleep well, my Beauty. I think I will. I love you. John

After 2 hr visit in Joan's home, late 5-12

Sent 5:30 a.m., 5-13
My Most Precious,

One thing for certain, holding you tight sure doesn't solve the sleep problem. I got home and could still sense your delicious scent, and once in bed I just lay there enjoying it. I think you said it is Tiffany?

I'm not even going to try to find words to tell you what those few hours meant to me, Joan. We could feel it in each other, love's purest light.

This will be a busy day, things a bit hectic at the office. I may not get back to you before bedtime but you know you're never out of my mind.

Warm kisses,

John

Sent 1:47 p.m., 5-13
Oh, John, I slept like a baby, and woke up feeling absolutely wonderful. Your love wrapped around me gives me a sense of peace and joy. I'm glad you could tell it was flowing both ways. I could, too.

You wrote that at 5:40 A.M.? You must be exhausted. I have been thanking God every few minutes for giving me you and an evening like that with you. I will add prayers that you will be able to get some rest today and sleep well tonight.

You are indeed the best kisser, the best hugger and the best back rubber. How did I get so lucky? I love you. Joan

Hi, again,
Dumb Question 1: Do you sleep with your hair down? DQ 2: How long to put it up in the a.m.?

Not-so-dumb Question: Were you *really* comfortable on that couch? I'm concerned about your back and I'm thinking you'd put up with some discomfort just to be nice to me. Let's be sure about that next time, okay?

I've had a couple of short naps on my office couch today, not very sound ones, as I can't get your face and that incredible hair out of my mind. Tonight should be better.

Sleep well, Sunshine. How I do adore you!

John

Sent 10 p.m., 5-13
Believe it. I sleep with my hair up because I would get all tangled up in it if I didn't. I take it down in the morning, brush it and put it up again. It takes no more than five minutes.

I was so happily comfortable in your arms last night that it doesn't seem a problem to me to be on that couch. I wanted to be there. I sit there alone a lot, reading or watching TV. It felt *so* much better with you beside me. Let's do it again and soon.

You must be in bed by now. I hope you are sleeping peacefully and will read this when you wake up. I am on my way to bed and will think of you, pray for you and dream of you all night with love.

Sent 5:15 p.m., 5-14 (Sat)
Hi,
Sweetheart, I suppose you are accustomed, by now, to wearing your (incredibly beautiful) hair the way you always do. But know this, I've been around enough by now, with my eyes open, to think that you are an eye-stopper wherever you go, and that beautiful silver mantle has a lot to do with it. So there!

Sleep well, love you.

John

Sent 7 p.m., 5-14
John, I made a pact with myself to come in from my yard work at seven and "talk to you." You sounded frustrated on the phone

and I wanted to make it better. I may not be the one to do so under the circumstances, but I need to connect with you no matter what.

I went out to squirt weed killer on individual dandelions etc. first. Boy, do I have dandelions. Then got into some weeding in my much too natural garden. Tomorrow Libby and I will probably plant the pots we didn't get done last week. I am so behind on gardening this spring . . . too much other stuff occupying my mind. YOU for one, two, and three, at least.

When you asked me what we were singing tomorrow, I went blank. I had been singing it or humming it all day. It is a very simple song with a lovely melody. You probably have not heard it, but then, our Choir Director is a Lutheran, so who knows? We sing the same words over four times, once only humming. It is perfect for Pentecost Sunday. It goes like this and is titled,

"If You Believe And I Believe"

If you believe and I believe, and we together pray,
The Holy Spirit must come down and set God's people free.
And set God's people free
And set God's people free
The Holy Spirit must come down,
And set the God's people free.

You and I believe, but we forgot to pray together Thursday; because we were so into each other. I thought of that the next morning.

Pentecost at my church is a big deal. Last year, a group of artistic ladies, (I was not among them) created a fabulous decoration for the day. It is huge and is placed above and behind the Chancel Choir. The center section in blues, white and silver is an image of a dove. It is surrounded by flames in red, orange, gold and silver. The choir is seated slightly above the Chancel and beneath the new very large and impressive pipes of our new organ. The "decoration" creates Ooh's and Aah's when people come into the Sanctuary. It must be on a permanent backing in sections, they were installing it again on Thursday night when I went to choir practice. The congregation is asked to wear flame colored clothes on this day. I used to do that, but now I wear the purple choir robe.

I may have written more than one page tonight. I'm not sure yet, but I thought this might sooth your troubled spirit. I will pray for your peace of mind and steadily improving health. I love you so. Joan

Sent 11 a.m., Sun 5-15 (Pentecost)
You are absolutely *The One* to do so, who else could??

I thought about our prayer omission on the way home and felt bad about it for awhile. My fault, actually, I know that the *man* is supposed to lead in these matters but I also know about forgiveness, as do you.

This will be a tough week at the office and I'm a bit concerned about tomorrow's session with my urologist.

Please pray that my bladder stents come out (about 11:15, give or take) without incident and that there won't be any debilitating after effects. More bleeding is always a possibility.

Swallows are building a nest in the box I put out for the chickadees!! First time I've seen them since mid-March. The box is on my little porch, very close and visible. So that's *very* good news. Nature's wonders continue to inspire me, and it's fun to try to "help" Her, even just a little bit.

Thanks for your beautiful description of your Pentecost motif and celebration. I love that kind of artistry, especially by Christian hands. I was to have read Peter's Pentecost sermon today, but I found a sub at the last minute.

That was a very touching and uplifting note you sent me, my Sunshine. Thank you so very much. My, how I do love you. John

Sunday afternoon, 5-15
John, this is the first possible time I have had today to sit down at the computer. Choir practice, the church service followed by coffee and a presentation of "Unsung Heroes," which is an acknowledgement of service and commitment to the church. They publicly name a few eager beavers once a year. I had my turn two years ago, I think. After that, I went with my "gang" to our usual hang out for breakfast. Libby was here doing laundry when I got home. The weather wasn't appealing for gardening, so we just visited. She left a few minutes ago.

I hope today is better for you. I have been praying a lot for that. I am glad if my note last night eased your pain a little. Here you are, having undergone surgery recently, coping with weeks of chemo, but staying on course, doing your church duties, keeping up with fishing trips, your job, and ME with no complaints that I have heard. I admire you for that, as well as many other things about you that cause my admiration. I hope that getting rid of those stents will make a big difference and that the process will not be difficult. You know I will pray for that today and tomorrow.

Today I was reading an article in the paper about Mt. St. Helens. It said she has a near twin on Russia's Kamchatka Peninsula, a 9,455 foot peak called Bezymianny. I knew approximately where it was because of you. I told you, you are stretching my mind. Another connection. I would never have had a clue before.

I connect with your love of the beauty of God's creation. I stand in awe of the plant and animal life on this earth. I'm glad you have residents in your bird box to enjoy up close. You and I feel the same way about so many things, John. It warms my heart.

I will understand if my e-mail goes blank this week, but I won't like it. Please let me know the aftermath of the stent removal. I'll be loving you and praying for you. Joan

2:05 p.m., 5-16
Hi,

I got home from my Monday at the church a little while ago. I was so glad to get your upbeat message on my answering service. What good news that is. I did a lot of praying during the morning, and I thank God that it went well and you feel better. I saved the message, so I can listen to your voice when I am missing you. There are a lot of those moments.

ILY

Sent 8:30 p.m., 5-16
Amazing! That volcano's name, as you spelled it in the transliterated Russian, means "Nameless." (Odd?) There are many active volcanoes along the Kamchatkan spine and it's not surprising that one of them would be much like Mt. St. Helens. I saw part of that range from a helicopter one sunny day, 1994, I think, incredibly beautiful!

Now, your interest in something like that leads me to an idea I've thought about since Thursday evening when you showed me the Geneve-provided Jr. Hi. test score results: Joan at the top of her class and John rather down the list. I spoke, if you recall, about IQ. I would bet a lot of money that if you and I took a standard IQ test right now, you would out-point me, and trust me, Dear Lady, this is no "line." Tell you why: IQ is really a measure of what one does with the cognitive wherewithal that God gave him/her. School age girls mature faster than boys and I should have looked more carefully to see the sex distribution on that page. But as adults, probably especially Seniors, someone like you would be ahead of someone like me because of what you're *doing* with your mind. And I continue to be amazed at your range of interests. You are one smart cookie, my Sunshine, and my oh my, does my love for you ever notice that!!

So, our "agenda" expands weekly. Maybe you could hire me ($1/yr) as your gardener, one visit a week. By age 85, who knows—??

Speaking of legal, I want to write next about your epitaph, "All I wanted was to be good." I'm searching scripture and I think I like what I see, relative to our love for each other. Not quite there, yet, but getting close.

ILY

Sent 10:25 p.m., 5-16
Dear best friend and my love,

I love your inquisitive mind. You are way ahead of me and that is O.K. I don't pursue knowledge as intensely as you do, but I do enjoy learning from you. You seem to know about every subject I have mentioned. I think you have a retentive memory which I've never felt I had. Age is making it even worse. I do love the English language, and for a couple of years got myself a meager do-at-home job, being a "Green Lady" for Mercer Island High School. I was one of a group of women who corrected the kids' English papers. It was tedious work, but interesting to me. There were some beautiful essays from kids I knew, but no one was allowed to know who any of the Green Ladies were. I must have done well because the English Dept. head asked me to work for her alone. I couldn't continue because, by then, my mom was living with me, and I had too much on my plate.

Tomorrow Morning at Nine O'clock I will finally be in the dentist's office to start work on the crown I will be getting for the tooth that broke off in California. I'll be home with my sore mouth right after.

Wednesday is busy. That is the Annual May Luncheon for all the Guilds of the Bellevue Arts Museum at the Seattle Tennis Club. I'll have to be over there around 10:40 for last minute preparations. I have to preside, introduce speakers etc. I should get home by 2:30.

I would love to have you as my weekly gardener. I might even pay $2.00 a year, but I couldn't guarantee that we would get much gardening done! It warms my heart to think of the possibilities.

ILY2, Joan

Sent 4:30 p.m., 5-17
Hi,
Playing phone tag with you this morning, left one msg but hung up on two other tries. Frustrating, isn't it?!

I prayed for you while you were in the dentist's chair, and I'm wondering how you'll wield your gavel tomorrow if you're still hurting. (Do you use a gavel, or just smile them all to quiet?!) What a Lady, *in charge*. I like that a lot.

Actually, my memory isn't as retentive as I'd like it, but I work with sometimes-complex material often enough that I know *patterns*. When I need details I can't recall, I ask someone or look it up. I already know that asking you is a lot of fun and I can learn so much from you. What a blessing!

Unrelated but maybe-important question: Have you ever traveled in a motor home? Somehow you don't seem like a "motorhome person," but I thought I'd ask. They're fun if you use them with some imagination and there are plenty of interesting destinations not too far off. I haven't used mine for quite a while, it sits in storage and I drive it around the block now and then, just to remind it that it's mine! But I think about that kind of "travel" now and then. So your curiosity can play with that, unless you reject it out of hand. (Imp John, again.)

Have a *great* day tomorrow with your gavel, or however you do that!

Many kisses, John

10:45 a.m., 5-17
John, I was happily surprised to have your message on the phone when I got home. It is true comfort. It was a rough hour and a half. My mouth is small and it really aches when I have to keep it open for so long. All better now.

10:20 p.m., 5-17
Yes, my Dearest, I do try. Sometimes I'd like to come down on their heads with a gavel, but mostly I bang a spoon against a coffee cup or glass and hope they pay attention. As a rule, this is a pretty casual group, which over many years has accomplished a great deal. They tend to all be Chiefs, no plain ol' Indians, which is always a problem among the people I know. Everyone thinks she is in charge. I guess we have all taken our turns at that.

I am still sitting here organizing what to say and how to say it tomorrow. I am getting tired and think I will head for bed and get up when you do to finish the tag ends in the morning.

You, blessedly, have been paying a lot of attention to me, and I am grateful. My mind is on you so much of the time I don't understand how I accomplish anything else, but I love it when you call or send messages. Love it more when I see you in person.

No, I have never traveled in a motor home. I can see that for an avid fisherman, it is perfect. Your ideas stir my imagination and my curiosity might get the best of me. Who knows?

ILY

Sent 9:15 a.m., 5-19

Good morning,

My, how you have spoiled me. After overcoming near-panic when my office computer failed (three times) to boot up this morning, I found no morning greeting from Joan. (I'm not supposed to use this computer on Uncle's time, but as I'm the Boss I can cheat just a little. Most of our "connections" go into my personal laptop.) It took a minute or two, but I then remembered, "Hey, Stupid, the Lady told you she was exhausted." Hope you went to bed very early and got caught up on your rest.

I was able to mail something to you yesterday, hope you'll find it interesting.

More as I can, My Love.

John

Sent 9:00 a.m., 5-19
Subj: Rest
Good morning to you, too. I was sitting at the computer, reading some of your old messages, waiting for you to make contact. Now I can face the day. I went to bed at 11:30, slept till 9:00 a.m. except for a couple of hours around four when I lay awake thinking of you.

Sent 11:30 a.m., 5-19
Subject: Scent (Yours)

To an unaware Martian, what follows would sound ridiculous. To you, I hope, less so.

I think we have learned an important lesson, in two parts:

1. That scent you were wearing Thursday night, whatever it is, was/is magnificent and goes perfectly with how I think about you and long for you.
2. It lingers in my clothing.

82

Which leads to a small story via Kamchatka. (Please follow this.) When we were fishing there in 97-98 it was common to see Brown Bear tracks in the soft river sandbars; they were anywhere from 10 to 14 inches long, BIG animals. But we rarely saw one as they pick up one's scent and leave quickly. There's an old parable, I think it's Native American: "A pine needle fell to the forest floor. The eagle saw it; the deer heard it; the bear *smelled* it."

Now, my office's admin officer (she's 50-ish and we would collapse like a wet tent without her) has a bear's nose. When I came into work last Friday morning, never thinking twice about wearing the same shirt as the night before, and even before I got into my little "executive" cubicle, she called to me (with everyone else listening): "Ah-ha, Mister Boss, and just where were YOU last night?!" She's so funny, most of the time, and so darned essential, that she gets away this kind of stuff all the time and we all love her for it.

But, seriously, I don't want my office staff to start nosing into my "social" life, *with you, is what I mean.* At my age, they have every reason to continue believing that I'm beyond romance, even "dating," and I'd just as soon keep it that way. So, a solution I hope you'll consider, and I don't want you to *not* use that stuff; just do what you do, as you did Thursday night.

Solution 1: I go to a shop and buy a jog suit, or something like that, decent enough to wear around your house and it stays with you. This precludes welcoming hugs at the door but maybe we have to give up a little spontaneity while I change quickly in your guest bathroom. Same just before leaving.

Solution 2: We only hold hands and kiss without hugs, back rubbing. Not so hot, methinks.

Solution 3: No scent. As noted, I don't like that much, either.

Having re-read what I just wrote, I really can't guess how you're going to react and I'm ready for just about anything (short of canceling your subscription).

Goodness, but I love you and miss you,

Me

Sent 12:03 p.m., 5-19
Dear John,

Whatever it takes. I am laughing again at this crazy situation we have put ourselves in. I have thought about that, too, because I know how perfume clings. The fragrance is "Tiffany," and I wear it all the time. I got it first when it had just come out. People stopped me on the street to ask what it was, so I decided it was my scent, forever. I am glad you like it.

Love, Smelly

Sent 4:15 p.m., 5-19
John,
I am astounded by your ability and the depth of your talent. I loved reading the article you sent. You put me right there in that river with you. I want more of the things you have written. The more I learn about you the deeper my love for you becomes. You are absolutely amazing to me. Yes. I have kept the brochure about Kamchatka. I just read it again. I am proud of you for being instrumental in getting those fisheries open. You have made a difference in this world in many good ways.

P.S. If you want to become a quick change artist, I'll go with that, so I can share my scent with you.

Sent 4:30 p.m., 5-19
Hi, Smelly (that's *awful* !),

Hey, gotta share this with you, just in from the BIG Boss Back East. This will sound a bit juvenile, maybe, but I just received a very enthusiastic "Attaboy" for the work my group has been doing recently on a very tough-to-address subject, always some angle in our counter-terrorism project. These kudos are *very* rare as the management seems to keep our team pretty well isolated from the others (there are three more, scattered around the country) and so long as we hear nothing about our work we are to assume that it's okay. Feedback from the people we write for (overseas outlets) is rare and a constant problem for the Boss who wants to help us evaluate our work. He's new (January) and aggressive and is a breath of fresh air.

I've known him for a long time and I recruited him into our Service nearly twenty years ago. It was he who persuaded me to take this "temporary" gig in the Northwest. We like and trust each other completely, and naturally that means a lot to me. I've told him, out of channels, of course, that I'm in touch with you as time and circumstance permit and he's happy to see me slowly crawling out of my hermit cocoon!

Have you ever tried going to bed at 9:30, *vice* 11:30?!

Whatever, do rest well tonight. But I know what it's like to wake and day-dream, rather tough on 75 year olds, don't you think? What *is* going on here??

Love you, endlessly

John

Sent 5:15 p.m., 5-19
Addendum: Thanks so much for the ready acceptance of my solution about your personal-forever scent. How long ago did you discover it? I bought my mom a silver (plated) brooch at Tiffany's in New York when I was in high school. She cherished it til the day she died. I'd give it to you if I could find it.

Dream well, my Beautiful.

Thanks for the kind words about the Kamchatka piece. That's a good example of how real leaders can take an idea and run with it, and I was able to watch that happen while being a part of the early steps. I'll share that story with you, of course!

Clue: A Russian (not Soviet) flag flying under the Stars & Stripes on my bachelor pad flagpole while I hosted in a key Russian fisheries scientist who came here to talk about the beginnings of what you read in that brochure! Wonderful few days, shuttling back and forth between UW Fisheries Department and Olympia fish management offices.

Once more, a blessed evening and good rest to the most beautiful and wonderful person on God's glorious earth!

A.M., 5-20 I've been thinking about your question the other night, about my "relationships" with other women in my many years of bachelorhood.

I finally became a Believer at about the time I was trying to save my marriage, but it was not enough. I eventually dated other women, of course, but my heart really wasn't in it. I suppose I didn't feel the need for "companionship," and nothing came my way that was even close to real love. Maybe my recollections of you, and my heartache over not aggressively pursuing you at the U-Dub, had something to do with this.

I can't deny that I occasionally thought about a sexual encounter, I was still in my 40's, after all, but it just never happened. By then I was really into the Scripture and had learned about "fornication," and "lust" and the rest of it.

You might find this hard to believe, but I honestly have *never* "lusted" after you, Joan. Your position on that pedestal of mine (remember, "Goddess"), always precluded that and it still does. I just wish we had had a few more dates in college so I could

86

have shown you that: no hanky-panky, ever. You were always way above that stuff in my heart.

As for adultery, I never came close while I was married. And nowadays I'm reminded that the biblical definition requires sex. Age and surgery have pretty well taken care of that option for me, maybe for you, too. Even if we were to go to bed together some day it would have to be mostly hugging. Not that I don't have those "long-suppressed feelings" but I don't *need* to satisfy them to love you with all that I have.

I guess this is easier to write than to say. I pray you'll understand.

Thanks for 'listening.'

Sent about 10:30 p.m., 5-19
Here I am again, beloved, still on my late night schedule. I doubt if I have ever gone to bed at 9:30 except before teen-age unless I was sick. Some people are just night people. Funny, we are similar in many respects . . . not this.

Do you realize you have sent me 7 e-mails today? I have been in seventh heaven to feel so connected. I have tried to answer as much as I could, but I know I didn't tell you that I shared your pleasure over the kudos from your boss. After reading what you sent me today, I know you deserve every accolade possible. You are so GOOD!

Did you get the Kamchatka thing back? I thought I sent it.

No wonder your mom cherished your gift of a silver Tiffany brooch till she died. What a lovely and loving thing for a high school boy to do. I can't remember when I first got my perfume. Must have been more than 10 or 15 years ago. Cliff gave it to me for some occasion and when I liked it so much he kept me supplied. In fact, after he died, Libby found a package of it in the trunk of his car waiting for an occasion. It had gotten damp and the wrapping was spoiled, so she took it to Tiffany in Bellevue, told them the story and they rewrapped it and I got it for Christmas 2003. Then, last year my sister and nieces pooled their money and got me a bottle for Christmas 2004. So you see, everybody knows it's me. Enjoy.

I loved the subject Us—you and me. I want it to be "us." You have been thoughtful and prayerful, and know that God blesses our love. It is so intense for me that I cannot ever remember having feelings like this. I want to be with you and right now it is hard to do. I treasure every moment. All day I have been thinking about one week ago today. I've been thinking that it seems ages ago. Too long. I'm not very good at hiding my feelings, John. I want to tell the world that this wonderful man loves me.

Now, one reason I am writing so much tonight is that I am going to be busy most of tomorrow. Of course, I had Choir tonight but these rehearsals will be ending soon because of summer schedule. But tomorrow I have exercise at 9:15. Go to Costco to get gas immediately after cuz I am almost empty. Rush home, change clothes and go to be a bridge substitute for a friend from 11:30 to probably 3:00. Then I go home, change clothes again and leave for a dinner party by 4:30. My friend for whom I did the Memorial Reception is taking a group of us, who did a lot for that, to dinner and as a thank you, at the Women's University Club. There will be four couples and me. I think she is planning something special.

In any case, I will check my e-mail when I can squeeze it in. I might even write a little. Today was such fun, I didn't want you to think I was deserting you. No way. You are always on my mind. I love you, now and forever.

Sent 4:30 p.m., 5-20
Joan,
Where do you get the energy for a day like today??!! I tire just thinking about it. Monday I start regular visits to my health club. The re-hab will probably be slow but I know it will work. No internal bleeding now for four straight days, what a joy that is!!

Hmmm, "four couples and me. I think she is planning something special," you wrote last night.

A wry smile creeps over my face as I think about that: If I'm this friend of yours, I'm going to have an eligible 70-ish bachelor as a sixth, probably a handsome widower whom you already know.

I confess to very mixed emotions at the very thought. We've talked about this before, you'll recall. Just remember, your long-term happiness is what matters most to me, no matter how that comes about.

A busy but stressful day for me. Tried to buy a jog suit but the pants are too long as I've shrunk top-to-bottom (haven't we all)? I'll stay after it, still hoping for a couple hours with you, maybe Thursday.

Your long note last night was such a wonderful read, Joan, I just melted into your heart as I read it, again and again and again. You are such an absolute jewel!!

How I do love you,

John

Sent 5-20, 8 p.m.
PS: I meant ninth (4 x 2 + 1, right?), not sixth. But maybe I'm being a little paranoid. How I ache to see you. Why does only a week ago seem so long?
ILY, madly. John

Sent 8:45 p.m., 5-20
PPS: I'm obviously too tired to be writing anything that requires math. 4 x 2 + 1 + 1 more = 10, So I should have said "tenth." But I really shouldn't have brought it up at all. Only one glass of wine, Dear Lady, you see what's going on here?! I want to put my head on your lap and close my eyes and just take in your

Tiffany. You're seeing my loony side a bit, I fear. Sleep well, for the both of us. xoxoxo

Sent 9:27 p.m., 5-21
Calm your fears. There was no rich bachelor present at the party. It turned out there were twelve of us, all people I know well. Two of us are widows. It was special. We were secluded in the WUC library for cocktails and many special hors d'oeuvres. I had a straight up vodka martini. Dinner was in the dining room with other diners there. There was live music and some people danced. We selected what we wanted from the menu. The hostess had special flowers on our table. She did very well considering that it has been so recently that she lost her son. This was a really big thank you for our efforts to provide the memorial reception for her son. Most of these people are Presbyterians. Believers.

I was home a little after nine and came right down to the computer to see if you had written. I was missing you, but I feel better now. I am glad the bleeding has stopped. Even when you have been told it is to be expected, it is unnerving. The exercise will build you up again. You know I am a great believer in that. It may take a little while, but it will come. I have been amazed that you went on two fishing trips while you were still recovering. I think you are either strong, determined or both.

Now about your multiplication and addition. How would I know if it's wrong? I don't do math.

I wish you *were* here with your head in my lap, relaxed and peaceful. Togetherness is hard to achieve except in our hearts and our thoughts.

I hope you are sound asleep as I write, dreaming of me. Thanks for your loving note. A perfect end to my day. I love you.

Joan

11 a.m., 5-21

I didn't say he had to be *rich*, just *available*. Right now, I'm afraid I'm neither, but you knew that going in!!

More later.

Imp

Sent 4 p.m., 5-21 (Sat)
Hi,

Take your time reading this. It will definitely remind you of your dad and of Cliff. One of Medved's better pieces, in my opinion. If you're not familiar with Hillsdale College remind me to tell you about it.

Love you,

John

Sent 4:30 p.m., 5-21
John, I do know about Hillsdale College. I get *Imprimis*. I read what you sent, wondering why I hadn't seen it before. It was in a stack of stuff piled on my kitchen table waiting for me to get around to it. So I read it all.

This has been a lazy day for me. Guess I am recovering from yesterday. I paid some bills, read newspapers that had piled up, but kept thinking I should be outside tending my yard. Somehow the weather did not call me out there. My energy level will probably be back to normal tomorrow. I hope.

I loved talking to you. I always do. XOXOXO

Sent 8:40 p.m., 5-21
I have known *no one* who gets *Imprimis*, certainly no ladies. So why am I not surprised to learn that you are the exception!? God *must* give us ten more good years, my Sunshine, to explore all of our common threads. Amazing!!

I wonder if you and Cliff ever received or knew about *Contentions,* a monthly newsletter published by Midge Decter (Norman Podhoretz' wife) during the Cold War. Brilliantly anti-communist, tough, humorous, biting. Some of the best neo-con writing I've ever read. She's over 80 now, still writes now and then. We owe a lot to these Jewish-Americans of the Medved stripe and I think Midge Decter was/is hands-down the most effective and influential woman of the bunch.

What kind of vodka was it? You said high-quality, as I would expect. Stoly is pretty good and they price it as though it had better be. Some of the Finnish brands are probably just as good. We'll have to have a little glass clinking (your martini in view, of course) one evening when neither of us has to drive. E.g., motor home "adventure."

My, it was great to talk to you this morning. Have others (men, especially) commented on your voice? It is just so fascinating: sexy, alluring, lovely, cultured. How do you do that? Come to think of it, I think I remember it that way before you became an adult. Not all of this is prejudice, believe me.

I'm pooped. Did an hour's light weeding in my little bird sanctuary, felt good. I'll sleep well tonight and try to dream of you. I usually dream of nothing, darn it, so you're not being discriminated against. The few times you've been in my dreams, they have been unforgettable. Like the ski resort, like Vienna.

Sing a note or two just for me tomorrow, my most Precious One. I'll hear it in my heart. I love you so. John

8:50 p.m., 5-21

My Dearest, I was sure you would be pleased that I receive "Imprimis" monthly. It is always fun to discover more things that connect us. I don't know anything about "Contentions" or Midge Decter though. If you have anything she has written, send it to me.

As for the vodka, "Stoly," yes, and sometimes there was some brand of Finnish. I even gave Cliff special glasses for iced vodka. I still have them but haven't used them for years. They are small and I think we used them at the dinner table when we had parties. Does that sound right? Sounds dangerous to me now, maybe even then. Would you like to have them? You could take them on your fishing trips. Class in the wilderness.

I am glad you had the energy to work in your yard. Wish I had. It is only 9:40 now and I think I will head for bed. I could use at least eight hours for a change.

There are times during my days when I am sure you are thinking about me. I feel like I am filled with your love from the top of my head to the tips of my toes. I hope you feel the same way from the love I am feeling for you. I will think of you as I sing tomorrow. I think God will allow a little space for you. I hope so. I love you. Joan

I sent her Alex's "Tel Aviv" piece 1:30 p.m., 5-22

Sent the Midge Decter piece about 2:15 She sent back saying she couldn't open it, I replied with suggestions.

Sent about 5 p.m., 5-22

Hi,

I first met Alex when he was "just off the boat" as a brand-new Russian-Jewish immigrant from the USSR, in 1974. He spoke no English but knew a lot about Soviet micro-chip technology, in those days a hot intelligence item, and so I interviewed him, in Russian and over a period of at least a year. He provided us with a lot of very useful intel. Over the years we became good personal friends, I eventually revealed to him my real identity (he still calls me "Bob" sometimes, much to our mutual giggling) and we're still very much in touch. His English now is a lot better than my Russian, he flies a Cessna 180 (takes me to lunch in it sometimes) and is just a great guy. More about him from your couch.

You need not *hope*, Sunshine. You can be *certain* that I'm thinking of you almost *always.* It's a problem for me, actually. Hard to concentrate on supervising, writing assignments, sermons, Mariners games, you name it! But are you ever worth it! Without understanding it exactly, I've been waiting 55 years for these times.

And I've *got* to close. Office weekend review approaching fast. More Monday. How many kisses can I squeeze through this e-mail?? Not nearly enough. Sleep well, my Beauty.

John

7:40 p.m., 5-22
John, It's me again. After I sent you the first brief message, Libby came over to help me with the planting. We worked pretty hard and accomplished quite a lot. Fortunately the rain squalls had quit so we had some dry time to work. At about six she wanted to go out to dinner so, we went down to a local restaurant. I paid this time because she had worked so hard.

You always are telling me you will elaborate on things you tell me when we get together, but then there is never enough time. I keep thinking of things I want to know about you and your life. I have a pretty good idea about 1st grade through 11 but, beyond that there still is a big void.

1. When did you get married, what was the wedding like, where was the first place you lived?
2. What kind of training did you go through when you chose your career?
3. Where were you stationed first, second, third etc.? How was life in those different places? Were you happy?
4. When were your kids born? Do they remember living in foreign countries? Did they like it? Are they as smart as you?

5. How long has it been since you lived overseas?
6. What did you do after you came back for good?

Those are only a few of the things I want to know. I think I tell you more about me than you tell me about you. I can tell what *kind* of a person you are and that is impressive to me. If it weren't, I wouldn't be in this place I am now. That just makes me want to know you better and better.

Am I being a snoop? I'll tell *you* anything you want to know . . . and probably more. Sorry I was sort of unavailable today. I meant to get this off before you went to bed, but it is probably too late for that. I am dreaming of Thursday. Love you, Joan

Sent 3:30 p.m., 5-23
No, no. No "snoop" at all. That's why we need ten years!

Okay, to your "test." September 14, 1951, in the bride's sorority house, my mom's Presbyterian pastor officiating. The bride comes down the circular staircase, everyone oohs and aahs. The groom is standing nervously at some distance and freezes, cannot smile as bride approaches. For this he was never forgiven and reminded of same *many* times. Not a good beginning. Twenty-four hours on train to D.C. via Chicago. Enter on duty with CIA 24 Sept. Many wedding gifts lost in shipment to D.C. but bride fails to thank most of the givers anyway, much to everlasting chagrin of groom's mother. Groom wonders about this. Not a good beginning at all. Remember, as I have explained, this is a *carnal* attraction.

We lived in a small apartment in Southeast D.C., two floor walk-up, two or three bus connections to work, in those days not far from the Lincoln Memorial, in old WW I "temporary" buildings strung along the Reflecting Pool. I learned to read the *Washington Post* with one hand looped around a standing-room-only bus strap.

A lot of early-on training, pretty heady stuff. But this I really must talk about, not write, and will be more than happy to do so.

Postings to Tehran, Iran 55-60, Cairo/Moscow 62-66, many TDYs to Europe, North and East Africa, all in pursuit/defense of Soviet targets. Came back to Seattle in 71, retired there in 78, immediately back on contract until 92, then this present assignment, so more than 50 years all together. The earlier Seattle gig was in some ways the most challenging and difficult although Moscow was a tough act to follow. I went out there as deputy chief of station and had to take on the chief's role for awhile when our COS was kicked out (PNGd). BIG job, right under the ambassador's nose 24/7.

Joan, my work was so great, in all those years I can't remember getting up in the morning and not looking forward to the day. How many men can honestly say that? And this post-retirement and "temporary" gig right now, at my age? I know guys, much younger, who would die for this assignment.

Happy at home? A different question entirely. But that was my choice, wasn't it? God expects the *man* to choose wisely and to lead in family relationships. That's the way He wired us. I failed Him and my family. Only His forgiveness lets me live with that. And that's why it's so deeply frustrating for me as I ask myself over and over again about those fateful (for me) two months, May-June 1950, about *you*: "If only I had—" (tried harder).

Scott, born "54 in Bethesda naval hospital, was 4 months old when we went to Tehran. Mike was born there in '57 in the US military hospital. Smart? Sure, but not top students because they didn't work at it. Smart as I?? You're too kind. I've not been very wise in some very major decisions, have I?? Big difference between "smart" and "wise."

Pastor Mike is the apple of my eye. Scott, something of an estranged son nowadays. That's tough.

Mike's son Steven, 16, is bi-polar, we've just learned. His folks have had a rough time with him these past 18 months as Steve has been in a virtual lock-up in various state institutions in Minnesota. He's home now, with new meds and a lot of optimism. Something to pray about. This summer, at home, will be critical.

Both my kids remember Moscow fondly. They had great friends, played baseball and ice hockey. (I was the Little League "manager" for all of Moscow!) They knew nothing of the sorrow I was going through with their mother, nor did she, then.

In all the years I knew/lived with Colleen she never once said to me "I love you." Imagine that!? I said that to her many times, at first and for awhile, always the same reply: "I'm glad." When I confronted her about her pat response she'd ask, "What *is* love?" You see where this goes, I think. She was a man-hater, I learned too late, like her much-abused mother had been. Father often came home drunk, beat up his wife, then they'd "make up" in bed. Pretty awful.

Joan, that's not a very happy account, as I re-read this some time after writing it. More later, better, I promise.

Love you so much, Thursday still looking okay, I'll phone tomorrow morning. xoxox

Sent 5:30 p.m., 5-23
John, Thank you for sharing your joys and sorrows with me. That is what I want. It only makes us closer.

It is a bit after six. I have been gone all day. It has been so lovely outside that I wish I had been working in the yard instead of sitting at a bridge table since about 1:45. When I talked to you last night I said I was on my way to bed, then I remembered the bridge commitment and the fact that I had promised to bring a dessert. I went upstairs and baked a pie. Just can't seem to hit the sack before 11:30.

I'll be waiting for your call tomorrow morning. I'm counting the hours till Thursday.

I love you.

Joan

2nd Grade, 1937. Joan is first on left, front row; John, 2nd from left, 2nd row. Geneve is 3rd from right, 2nd row.

Joan's High School Portrait

John's High School Portrait

Tap Dancing at Middle Age

Flowers, A Stunning Arrangement

Witch

CHAPTER 8

Oh, What Tangled Webs

Hi,

Goodness, Joan, I don't know how much longer you can put up with my brain lock when I'm on the phone with you. I know I do it much better when those beautiful dark brown eyes of yours are within arm's length, sometimes a lot closer!

I should explain that I decided some time ago that my relationship with you is none of my colleagues' business, here at my office. They're nice people, *very* good at what they do, but they're also a bit nosey and curious about this 70-something "boss" they've recently inherited. So occasionally I have to shade the truth a bit to explain some of my comings and goings, phone calls from my tax-payers'-supported desk, etc., where you're concerned.

How does it go: "Oh, the complex webs we weave, when we practice to deceive." Who said that?

Can't wait til Thursday, hope I don't pop something in the meantime. First visit to Bally was good, yesterday, no strains or pains this morning. But what I really want is to join *your* exercise class! But I guess it's ladies only, yes, we can have our own private version.

Love you so very much, I'm a new man these past months, I hope it shows.

Millions of kisses,

John

Sent 5:30 p.m., 5-24
Hi,

Guess I lied, cuz here I am again.

You noted how "long ago" it was since *Thursday* (can we ever forget that day?) and I know the same feeling. For me, here is this girl/woman/matron/widow for whom I have yearned nearly my whole life, now suddenly warm and soft in my arms, eagerly responding to my hugs and kisses, and I to hers. It seems nearly impossible, yet it is blessedly true. I only wanted, just a few months ago, that you would *like* me enough to continue a relationship of some kind. And now this!! A love I've never imagined could be possible for me. I feel like I owe you the world, Joan. Don't pinch me to awake from only a dream.

Good night, my Beauty.

John

Sent 8:20 p.m.5-24 Titled: "Everything"
John, I am sick. I just wrote you an hour long message and deleted it instead of sending it. It is 9:00 P.M. I still haven't had dinner, so that now I will do that and then try again. I loved your sweet words. Hopefully, you will get my re-do in the morning. I am filled with love for you.

Joan

Sent 11:52 p.m.

John, It is after 11:30. I had my dinner finally, did dishes, put on my jammies, brushed my teeth, said part of my prayers. Now I will try again.

"Oh, what tangled webs we weave, when first we practice to deceive." Sounds like Shakespeare to me?

In my very long letter which I lost, I started by telling you that I had worked in my yard for at least six hours today. I think I started writing about eight o'clock. I thought I was tired then and probably wouldn't be able to move tomorrow. Now I think it may take a week.

However, men ARE welcome in my exercise class. We accept both sexes, all denominations, all colors, all ethnic groups, no charge. I have had two men at the same time. One was the husband of a church member who came to class. They came together for a long time. The other was not a Presbyterian. He had had both knees and hips replaced. He was very deaf. I made him stand right in front of me, so he could watch the way I moved. He was so happy there that he wrote a letter to the church about how great I was and gave them money. Unfortunately, he has since died. There are no men in the class now, but we would welcome you. Me especially. I guarantee that I will get you in shape for anything.

Another thing I asked in my former lost letter was would you please find me a snap shot or small picture of you as a mature man. I have looked up pictures of you in our HS yearbook and also in the "Tyee." Both have very nice images of you in your youth. I have always been partial to blue eyed blond men, but I would like to have something more current to put in my pocket. Also, bring me a picture of your parents to look at. You got to see mine. I have a vague recollection of yours but would like to have my memory refreshed.

The last thing I wrote about was church, and it was a very long paragraph. It was about the fact that since I have joined the choir I have discovered many things I did not know were a part of

Presbyterian worship. Cliff and I were very faithful Sunday church attendees. I was most often in some sort of Bible study, but I did not know about things I have discovered since I joined the choir. Some of them I know have not always been done.

On Ash Wednesday we get ashes on our foreheads. We do it at night, but we get them. I always envied Catholics who walked around all day with that sign visible for all the world to see. We also do anointing. A total surprise to me, and you can request it if you are dying. Lately, just in the past few weeks, we have placed the Baptismal Font at the entrance to the Sanctuary, now we have been told we may dip our hand into the water and cross ourselves on the forehead either on the way in or out. I love doing that. These symbols have always seemed important to me, but until lately Presbyterians have seemed a little cold in those respects.

Last Sunday we had 42 kids join the church. Six received baptism. The choir sang a swaying, clapping anthem which received rousing applause. What ever happened to those staid old Presbyterians in Sumner's big old brown church in which you and I first met Jesus?

Well, My beloved, it is 12:30. Off to bed to dream of those kisses to which I cannot help but respond. I love you, John, wonder of wonders. It is true.

Sent 1:30 p.m., 5-25
Hi,

I "ouched" when you said you'd zapped a very long letter. I can relate to that. Thanks for reconstituting it for me. I'm not surprised that you're better at Shakespeare than I am. Did you look that up or did it just roll off your tongue?

It's just about uncanny but I was thinking about you in church Sunday (no surprise) with respect to some of our Lutheran rituals. They're often quite similar to the Catholics,' as with your ashes on the forehead. We do that too. Once a month there's an anointing/healing service following Communion (which we have every week), prayers, oil, for those who want it. I've been up there twice, each time when I had just learned about my cancer problems (prostate, then three years later, bladder) and was kind of shaky. Very meaningful and helpful. Anyway, I was thinking you'd really enjoy one of our services, once you get the hang of the liturgy and the way the music fits in. It takes awhile for it to have real meaning, as it has now for me for many years. And I know you've discovered how much more all of these things mean when you're in some kind of regular study of the Word. I'm so thankful for my earlier opportunities to teach, teachers always get the most out of it.

The font and water became part of our service a few years ago and I don't know why it wasn't before. So far, I'm not entirely comfortable crossing myself, although I can't explain that. I'd say more than half of our congregation does not. Now that I know you do it, I may too.

And another thing I should mention, about my last Communion experience. I always have vivid memories, during communion, of my visit to "the upper room" in Jerusalem when I toured there some years ago. Don't know if I've told you this before, but the room is said to be very much like *the* room used by Jesus and His disciples on that Maundy Thursday evening, so long ago. It might actually be the room, no one knows for sure. I still can see it in my mind's eye and Sunday, in church and in some mysterious way, you were with me in that very room, we were holding hands and weeping gently together. I had to leave quickly after the service to avoid my emotional shock being seen by others, it was beautiful but embarrassing at the same time. And then, of course, during that part of the service, I replayed all the what-ifs about our relationship and my super stupidity regarding you when I was much younger. I hope I get all this emotional stuff out of my system before I start going to church with *you*.

Your church and mine must be on some kind of similar "schedule" as I celebrated Confirmation Sunday, which is a really big deal for Lutheran families with children. These kids are about 12, I think, and the pastor read some of their "faith stories" during his sermon. Very impressive stuff, makes this Old Coot feel pretty good about the future of our faith.

Six hours is too much garden time!! I hope you'll have a little energy left for tomorrow, at least enough to fall in to my arms.

I'm arranging the office workload so that I can escape for a few hours then—and please help me remember to pray, first.

I can't wait, but must. You are my absolute Everything, my dearest Joan.

How I do love you!

Sent 6 p.m.
Oh, John.

I have to wait almost 24 hours, but I think I can do it!

This morning was a convertible top down morning. After exercise class, I took stuff to the recycle, then drove to Bellevue to get some tomato plants at Lowes, did some other shopping at a drug store there that carries things I can't get on the Island. It felt good to be out in the fresh air.

When I got home I realized my hours of yard work yesterday were catching up. I read your message. It made me feel good, but I was too pokey to write. Had lunch, read the paper, took a little nap then got up to plant my tomatoes. There is so much to do in this big yard. I have only made a little dent.

I put some dinner on to cook, came down to connect with you via e-mail and behold a miracle. I am so excited that you will be with me tomorrow. I am ready to fall into your arms no matter what, but I think I will have regained my energy by then.

Sweetheart, It really touches me that you have these emotional dreamlike experiences in which we are together sharing special moments. I wish I *had* been there in that place with you. Communion at my church will be next Sunday. It is always on first Sunday of the month, and as I said before, I wish it were more often. It won't be long before we can share it. Don't worry about your emotions showing or trying to squelch them. I love you for it.

You make me feel so cherished. You used to tell me you wanted to help me. I told you that you do, but WOW, I never knew it would be this much. I love you, I love you, I love you.

Joan

John visited with Joan for two hours at her home, Thursday afternoon, 5-26.

Sent 8:30 p.m., 5-26
No way to say how much those two hours meant to me, we need to do this more often.

I pray I will always be worthy of and interesting to you, you're such a *force* in my mind and heart.

Beautiful, Beautiful Joan, how I love you. John

10:25 p.m., 5-26
I got home from choir practice just a bit ago. Hung around to chat for longer than usual, hopped into my top down convertible and left it that way for the drive home. It was still a little light out, and I feel pretty safe on Mercer Island. I won't do that off Island at night unless you are with me.

Good bedtime messages. Isn't that exciting? After you left I started thinking about what food I could provide. You get me all stirred up with your plan-ahead ideas. You suggested this as a possibility quite a while ago and said you would think about how to make it happen. Are you a wizard? There seems to be some sort of magic going on when I am around you.

Tonight was the last Thursday night of choir practice till Fall. We will go even earlier to practice Sunday mornings for the next two weeks. Then it is summer vacation. Next week in honor of Memorial Day, we will be leading the hymns, as usual, but unusual for Presbyterians any more, the hymns will be "Battle Hymn of the Republic," and "The Navy Hymn." They have to print the words in the program for the congregation because they are not in the Hymnal. The choir absolutely loves the "Battle Hymn." The following Sunday is the last time the choir will sing till September. Our anthem that day will be "How Lovely is Thy Dwelling Place" from the "Requiem," by Johannes Brahms. It is gorgeous and falls into the category of the Hallelujah Chorus. It is hard and we've been working on it for a long time, but we will make it. Too bad you can't come to church that day.

Thank you for giving me a lovely afternoon. I think I am energized by that wonderful back massage. It wore you out, but did the opposite for me. It is 11:15 p.m. and I am still very alert. I probably will be reliving all those together moments all night long. The more I learn about you, the more impressed I am. I loved hearing about your life. Keep on telling me. I want more and more.

Long tight hugs and long sweet kisses,

Joan

Sent 5-27, 7 a.m.
Hi,

I learned at least three *new* things about you yesterday, sort of in order of interest (to me):

1. You are even more beautiful than I remembered.

2. Your back is easily the most heavenly of all (2) backs I have now rubbed.

3. You endure warm temperatures better than I do.

1. This probably won't come across the way I want it to, but yesterday was the first time, ever, maybe, that I've seen you up close in bright sunshine (that word again). Out on the deck I noticed very keenly the "crow marks" around your eyes—that's the tricky part of this piece, we don't call them wrinkles—and I was struck by how much they show off your already-remarkable deep-brown eyes. I think most women regret the onset of these hard-won age badges but you should not; never. No "line," my Beautiful, you are one unique Lady and I continue pinching myself to say, "Yes, John, this is really happening to *you!*"

2. Your back. Hmmmm. No flab, for sure, I wasn't surprised at that, but I think it's strong and straight and, yes, 'noble." A back that belongs in that apparition on the Viennese boulevard. A back that would fit the 35-ish Joan I saw in that vision. And I could rub it for an hour straight without pause, but I have to keep reminding myself that I'm not at par owing to the recent chemo treatments. You haven't mentioned arthritis in your neck before. Is that painful, always? Have you tried the condroitin-glucosomine combo? I've been using it for years and believe it really helps.

3. Warm weather. Related to sub-par stamina, maybe, but I noticed the warm afternoon didn't seem to bother you at all. It did me and I'm thinking now that maybe my years in the Persian desert didn't acclimatize me as well as I thought. I'm also thinking that when you're in your next a bridge game—if you think about me as much as I do about you—you may have trouble remembering where all those cards are.

You mention "Battle Hymn," my favorite hymn and one that some know I want sung at my memorial. Trouble is I tear up when I hear it. This is something I inherited from my sensitive mom and have never been able to conquer. Some music just does it to me, can't help it. I even shed a few tears listening to the president this morning as he addressed the graduating

Annapolis grads (a fierce and moving speech, by the way). The national anthem, properly performed, the same. It has to do with fine art (music), country (fierce patriotism, uncompromising pride) and a few other things. I'm especially moved when reminded (usually in good sermons) of God's incredible free gift of grace and forgiveness and I know that has a lot to do with my not knowing Him until I was in my early 40s and how fortunate I am now.

"Dwelling Place" I don't think I know. The nearby Pres choir is better than my old Lutheran church, I think mainly because it has about 10 more voices. But the music choices are little more to my liking, even though I've been a Lutheran now for 33 years. So I'm sure I'd be overwhelmed by yours, which I won't get to hear, at least not before my contract runs out in October.

And speaking of my contract, my Boss-Friend in Washington has decided to do an inspection of our little group. He's new to his job and so that's not surprising. What *is* surprising, he's told me to "get lost" for the few days that he's here. He's not interested in inspecting *me* and he rightly figures my staff will be more up-front with him if I'm not around. Now is that a *blessing* or what??!!

So, this just in: Motor Home Rez No. 37654, Ocean Mist Resort (near Ocean Shores), June 29, 30, July 1, the days he'll be visiting my office. We probably won't use the 3rd night cuz I want to spend time in *your* world, too, but it's nice to have just in case. We'll want to get there as early as possible, best chances for a spot nearest the beach.

Yes, these things *do* usually happen with a little planning and "help." This note will have to do for today/tonight, my Most Precious. The office has just been directed to do a make-up assignment, a "Special" for our group in Dallas, and it's due Memorial Day. We haven't even started yet. This is too long for one sitting, but I couldn't help myself. I love you so, beyond words.

John

Sent 7 p.m., 5-27
Here's a smile-maker, before bed this warm Friday:

My motor home is "built for two," but I've been using it solo for quite some time. Now that will change. You'll get the bed in back, and I the couch in front, privacy screening in between. I think we can manage that, hmmmm?

What's your brand of gin, vermouth? I'll buy. Maybe you could bring a nice wine. We should have enough groceries on hand for the first day so we don't have to lose time getting there by stopping to shop. Can do that later in Ocean Shores if needed. Do you like fresh crab? If it's not a favorite of yours we should try something else and I'm not sure it's always available. This is a very special opportunity, let's not waste a moment of it!

Something to dream about, no?!
Gotta go, time's running out.

Love you, love you, love you

John

Late Evening, 5-27
John, I love getting a nice long message. It gives me lots of thoughts for answers. Today I am so filled with you that it really is hard to keep my mind on the task at hand. I couldn't believe I got through the exercise class without saying your name out loud. The feeling of being in your arms was steadily there as I called out the exercises by rote. I have somewhat different routines for each day. I followed "Friday" faithfully, but I didn't think I could make it. You were in my head the whole time.

This afternoon was just the same. I played bridge from 1:30 till close to five. Same problem. It could have had something to do with the fact that we didn't win, but at least, I didn't blow my cover.

Now about your #1. comment. Bless you. There is nothing I hate more than having someone take a picture of me when I am facing bright sunlight. You make all those "crinkles" seem acceptable. Thank you for that.

#2. My straight back is due to my Dad who walked around the dinner table at night and poked us between the shoulder blades and said, "Sit up straight." Posture has always been important to me. I tell my class that they will look younger if they stand straight. I always try. The arthritis in my neck is not often a bother. My back doctor told me it was there when I had an MRI for the back. I do take Glucosamine Chrondroitin every day, and it has truly helped me.

It feels cool down here at my computer, but it is really hot upstairs. Bridge today was in the home of my friend who has air conditioning. I had better get out my fans.

I can understand tearing up at music. It has emotional powers over me too. There is a man named Gordy in our choir. He and his wife are friends of mine. I went to their 60th wedding anniversary celebration last year. He was a pilot during World War 2 and then in the FBI. He has tears running down his cheeks over the "Battle Hymn," The "Hallelujah Chorus," and "How Lovely is Thy Dwelling Place," among many pieces of music he loves. I am glad that you respond that way as well.

It was my intent to get this to you before you go to bed tonight. I cannot imagine ever finding you uninteresting. The more I am with you the stronger it gets. It is scary, and my responses are beyond my control. You will have to help me with this.

I hope you will get this tonight. I love you.

Joan

Sent about 2 p.m., 5-28

I am taking a short break to cool off. Ate lunch on the deck in semi-sun. It was warm and felt good but now is a bit too hot. I still have to put water on all those pots.
There are about seventy so far. Still more to plant.

In answer to your question about my choice of gin and vermouth. I normally choose Gordon's. The reason for that is price and alcohol content. Tanqueray and Beefeaters are too strong. You don't need to buy gin when you will be drinking vodka. I can put some vermouth in a tiny bottle. I have Martini and Rossi on hand. I'll bring some olives, too. I'll look for some tastes-good reasonably priced wine.

I love fresh crab. We always have it on Christmas Eve, then a big dinner on Christmas Day. It seems to be more readily available in the winter. If we can find it that would be great. I'll bring lunch stuff, probably fruit and sandwiches and at least one dinner. What kind of food do *you* like best?

I think some of my close friends would be scandalized if they knew what I'm planning. So far only Libby knows that we're in touch. But I really do hope we can pull this off, John. It scares me a little, but I want it badly.

I want to send this now but the computer tells me to wait. There is a problem on the e-mail server. Nuts!

8 p.m., 5-28
Joan, I really do admire your willingness to go along with this plan, a bit out of your normal pattern, to say the least. I confess to being a bit awed myself at the opportunity. But we need *time* together, without rushing, and long talks and shorter walks are the answer. Besides, you'll see me in something of my own element and you need to be sure you still like what you see. E-mails are great but not the *real* thing.

I know you've told me that you and Cliff used to take your little kids to the beach, clam digging and the rest. I used to do that with my kids too, but gave up the clam shovel when my back couldn't take it any more. Seems that was a long time ago!

And I am *so* looking forward to doing *your* thing over the Fourth weekend, back at your MI home. I'm pretty sure the Boss will be here long enough for that to happen.

You're right about the crab. I need to phone down there and see if it's too far from winter. I'll do that.

On the wine, I thought you might bring a bottle or two that you like, from home. I don't want you spending all the money on this gig!

Gotta go, again. Time is fleeting.

I love you, Joan. How many ways to say it?

John

P.S. Your dad was a wise man but he also knew he had a budding beauty in his family. Your posture (I think I described your "regal gait") was very evident in my Vienna Vision, and after not laying eyes on you for decades. Go figure!!

Pinch me, or what??!!

ILY

John

Sent about 8:30 p.m., 5-28, Sat
My darling, this has been a terrible afternoon. I kept trying to connect but my server was down and no communication. I was afraid you would think I had deserted you which was the furthest

thing from my mind. It is 8:00 and I haven't had dinner yet because I kept coming down here to see if my message ever got through. Thank God it did. I will be able to sleep tonight.

I will be up early for choir rehearsal, church, then maybe brunch with the usual group. At 4:30 I will meet my friends who go together for dinner and the Issaquah Theatre for "Music Man," the last performance of the year. I know it will be good. I am so relieved that I finally connected with you. I talked to a friend about this many-hour problem. Her husband said it was MSN's trouble. They should fix it, but if not call them. I feel much relieved.

I hope you got both of the e-mails I sent.

I will pray tonight and in the morning that your cough will disappear, that you will read Genesis to completion with your usual aplomb and in the voice that sends shivers through me when you call.

John, when I feel disconnected, I suffer. I am so happy that I finally was able to hear from you.

I hope you feel wrapped in my love. It is there.

Joan

7:30 p.m., 5-29
Hi,

I've been at an anniversary party for Pete Soverel and his wife, all afternoon, in Edmonds. Missed you terribly, even when talking to many old fishing friends. Nothing else seems to matter to me any more. I had hoped to use this party as a means to drop by your place on the way home but an old friend asked to ride with me and I couldn't say no because there was no other way for him to get there. And then I know that Sundays aren't very good for that sort of thing.

Church was good—good read, no coughing, thank you for your prayers—but I saw you only throughout the service, even at the communion rail. Always before, only Jesus. I need to work on that!!

You sounded scared in your e-mails yesterday. That scared me, too. But the one that finally came thru was well worth the wait. We *share* our need to be connected, my Sunshine, we are each helpless about this. I've *never* felt like this before.

"Music Man," one of my favorites. Gotta go. I ache to be with you.

John

11 p.m., 5-30
Subj: Me Too
John, I just got home from the evening performance of "Music Man." I have tried to get a message off to you during the day, but it just wouldn't work. I went to church at 9:30 to practice and didn't get home till about two. Libby was here and still here when I left for dinner and the theater at 4:15. I thought even a brief goodnight note would help, but I was afraid she would pop down here and see what I was doing. Sorry. I've been aching, too.

I prayed for you last night as always, and again the moment I woke up, concentrating on the cough. I'm really glad you were coughless while you read.

If you had been at our church service today, I'll bet you would have ended up in tears. It was the best Memorial Day service we have ever had. The postlude was the "Star Spangled Banner" played in a wonderful, unusual arrangement on our fabulous new organ. The choir always sits and listens as the postlude is played while many people leave. Gordy, the teary guy, cried buckets. Most of us had tears in our eyes. Many people stayed.

Tomorrow morning I will go to the Memorial Service at Sunset Hills Cemetery in Bellevue. Did I tell you about that before? My sis and I will go and maybe one of my nieces. I will take red flowers. Barbara will bring blue and white. We'll put them together, divide them up and put some on the graves of my mom, my World War I veteran uncle, and his wife. Also buried there, a Korean War veteran cousin by marriage and his wife, my cousin. I love the service at this place. There are long rows of tall flagpoles with huge flags flying as you come and go. There is always a bagpipe band in kilts and tall black beaver hats. Veterans marching in uniform, singers, speakers and prayers, then a gun salute followed by the release of many doves who circle around us before flying home. We go every year. I may end up at either my sister's or nieces' house for lunch and not get home till afternoon.

The production of "Music Man" was terrific and the male lead at least as good as Robert Preston. It was fun all the way through, but the love story really got to me. I was seeing you and wanting to be with you. That seems to be a constant condition. I wanted you there beside me holding my hand.

I hope tomorrow will offer moments when we can at least send e-mails. I feel lonely and longing for you without, but they don't compare with being with you. How ever did this happen?

Good Night, my love, and Good Morning now as you read this. You are always in my heart which is FULL of love for you.

Joan

2 p.m., 5-30
Hi,

Did you know that I notice "firsts"?

Let the record (ours) show that on Sat., May 28, 2005, you first called me "My Darling." (Maybe a small "d," no matter.) I *really* like that and I think no one, except maybe my mom when I was very small, has ever called me that. I'm allowing that you were under the stress of MSN screw-ups, but that makes it all the more spontaneous and genuine, doesn't it? You probably used that term for Cliff, whom you loved very much. It doesn't matter, because *you* said (wrote) it. And I hope you'll say/write it again, often.

Joan, your description of your church service and your Memorial Day activities today absolutely touched me to the core. What a wonderful tradition you have with your church and your family. Lovely beyond words, again just tearing at me to be able to be with you. I've missed so much of you and yours over all these years.

Wrapped in your love. Absolutely, I feel it 25 hours a day. And it's reciprocal, isn't it? What have we done, my Beauty??!! I think we're giving each other something beautiful, even miraculous, in these later years. Not many so fortunate, we must be grateful to Him for loving us and allowing (causing?) this to happen.

Must go, wish it weren't so.

Words fail again, so much love to express.

John

Sent 6:00 a.m.
Believe it or not, I am up. Just thought I'd surprise you with an early morning greeting to make up for yesterday.
I love you, John.

6:10 p.m.
My Darling, (capital "D")

Barbara and I had coffee at Starbucks and visited for quite a while. Then she asked me to go with her to help select a gift for her granddaughter who will be graduating from high school in a couple of weeks. We both drove to the Bellevue Mall, parked side by side in the garage close to Nordstrom and shopped. When we got into our cars to go our separate ways, she opened her window and yelled, "Don't Leave!" Her car would not start. She called for roadside assistance, and I insisted on staying with her till help arrived. It took more than an hour. The helper got lost. I still don't know what the trouble was/is. She insisted I go home when he did arrive. Her daughter would get her if necessary. I'll check with her after I get off this machine. Maybe she has left a message by now. I think you are right about changing to Comcast. It would be nice to be on e-mail or the web and still get phone calls. It would be *very* nice if my messages got to you on schedule, especially when I make an effort to get up early and impress you.

I loved having your message when I got home. I feel together when I read your words or am writing mine to you.

I have thought a lot about going to my church together on July 3. I would love to have you meet my friends and come to our after-church brunch, but as we agreed the first time you came to my house, I think it's best not to. You're right, it would be hard for me to "explain" just who you are and what you do and that can all wait for a better time.

I do feel wrapped in your love. I know, beyond doubt, that this is a two way, reciprocal love that we feel.

I hope you get to read this before you sleep. I thank God that you love me. Goodnight.

Joan

4:30 p.m., 5-31
Hi,

Back to "on the beach" planning:

Food: grapefruit juice, cereal, bananas, V-8 juice, bread (your favorite, let me know), sandwich makings (we discuss this), soup(s) (many kinds aboard the MH). We check on the fresh crab in Ocean Shores the first day, if it's available and looks okay, then decide if we want a bottle of some kind of white wine which we can get at the Safeway at Ocean Shores, you choose, of course.

Bring our own gin/vodka stuff, w/ olives as you said.

Snacks (pre-dinner, w/ cocktails): we can talk about this.

Other stuff: Your overnight bag, whatever goes in there is your call, natch, just don't forget it as I won't have extra pajamas. Any favorite CDs, reading material (for while I take my 20 minute nap! Ho, Ho!).

I'll have clean towels, wash cloths, soap, etc. I'll bring a few kites, my laptop (with our "diary" in it, for you to quiz me on, if you wish), and the 98.9 smooth jazz CD, if I can find it here in my office. Would we spend any time watching TV? If so, I need to bring a satellite receiver, no problem, used to do it all the time, but my hunch is TV wouldn't command precious time, would it??

I'll bring some photos, Agency citations, etc., to prove to you that I really was a spook who did okay by all you tax-paying citizens. You might have some old pics, too, I'd love to see you in those.

Honestly, I don't know how you've put up with all the heartache over the years, my Beloved, just unreal. I hope my arms offer some comfort. I had never heard of Barbara's tragedy until today. My step sagged a bit when I got out of the car. Talk to me about it, all you want, if it will help.

So much to learn and know of each other. But He will provide, I'm convinced of it.

Must go. Endless love.

John

6:40 p.m., 5-31
Got your message, My Darling, and incidentally, *if* I called Cliff that, it was probably only when I wrote letters to him in Korea.

As for Monday. YES! Thinking about that first evening with you curls my toes. I have a strong sensation that this has been going on for a *long* time, yet when I check my e-mails, it has only been a few months. It is my fault for being so brazen that I told you I love you. I am glad you have responded to my declaration so warmly.

As for plans for our beach get-away, I need to know if you have any food allergies, strong dislikes, special likes, medical reasons for avoiding some things. I lived so long doing heart safe food, after Cliff had bi-pass surgery, that I tend to cook that way in general, but I am thinking that I will bring a couple of things that will last for more than one day, like a really good pasta salad and a really good broccoli salad that has bacon and onions etc. I could put together a yummy, simple chicken thigh thing to bake while we have our cocktail the first day. If we get crab, we can save the chicken for later. I want to have everything done ahead. I love to cook, but this trip is for us to spend time just being together, getting to know and understand each other more, and having fun. If we want dessert, we can buy ice cream. What is your favorite?
I hope I covered the necessary stuff for the moment. It is time for me to eat my dinner. I feel elated, excited, hopeful and a little apprehensive, all at once. But I will love it if we can really truly go hide away together at the end of June. ILY, Joan

5-31, Bedtime
Hi,
What a wonderful, encouraging e-mail, and before I go to bed. Oh, my, have you ever re-charged my batteries!!! Thank you, thank you, thank you, my Beautiful One.

I eat *anything* and from you will love every bite. No allergies, no hang-ups, just love for this incredible woman who loves to cook as well as loving me. Sorry, but I have to quit, much as I'd like to write to you all night. Big day tomorrow.

Me

Sent 2:30 p.m., 6-1
Sorry, I lied, or rather, forgot. I *don't* eat spicy-hot food and don't like those TV dinners that have too much pepper in them. But TV dinners we probably won't be doing, right?!

Add to your check list: *The Message.* Beach shoes to get wet, pants/slacks the same (likely to be too cool/breezy for shorts but bring some in case it's warm enough), there are some *small* creeks that are fun to wade across. Remember, even in June-July it can be breezy and cool, even cold if it's cloudy. This isn't Hawaii, but it's big and can be very private.

The chicken and salad ideas sound beautiful to me and this mobile pad of mine does have an oven that works very well, microwave too. How about coffee/tea? I can fresh-grind the beans if you like, although I have only Starbucks French Roast and you said once you don't like Starbucks as well as others. Lots of herbal tea on board. Ice cream: simple vanilla but with chocolate sauce and nuts and sliced bananas and I think that's a banana split, maybe too heavy? I'll bring the ice cream as I think we'll have some extra room in the freezer, unless you already have a favorite which I'm sure I'll like just because you do!!

Love you, my Precious, oh, so much!!

John

6:14 p.m., 6-1

I had another of my busy days. Led exercise and then immediately left for Bellevue and a two hour meeting at the Museum with the Bellevue Arts and Crafts Fair paid Coordinator and three other volunteer people beside myself who have long been instrumental in organizing this stuff. We were working on the Patrons Party, $75.00 per person. We are hoping for about 450 people and would like 600, but the Botanical Garden people are limiting us this year. That ticket price will not make us any money, it will only cover costs. I wish you could be my date. I wish a lot of things for us but will be always grateful for what we have which is very special to me. That's what love does, and I love you.

Joan

P.S. What *is* a TV dinner?

8:15 p.m., 6-1
Hi,
Love your spirit: "Secret get away," "hide away." You're getting there, my Most Beautiful, absorbing my "spook-ness." Not so sure I really want this of you, I love your guileless nature and often wish I could have more of the same, difficult after all these years in my chosen profession. I made the first big decision today, where to stash the MH while I fetch you. I wanted it close and quick so's not to waste time. There's a huge parking lot at the Puyallup fair grounds, empty this time of year, and right on our way. If you can put up with the Saturn for 35 miles, each way, we'll be in great shape. (It's a great fisherman's car!) You're going to learn a lot about me, my Sunshine, which is what we want, isn't it?? I'm like a kid, again, so excited. I have nothing to hide, I'm yours warts and all.

Instead of going to their monthly class luncheon, Joan stays at home and John joins her for two precious hours.

6-2, 9:20 p.m.
Hi, Sweetheart,
Incredible afternoon, you are such a classy person, even a simple sandwich is a masterpiece! I'm getting used to having you in my arms and I cherish every minute. We need many more.

I'm mad at myself for forgetting to ask you if that CV is a copy you can give away. I'd like to have it and go over it with you as some of the things I don't understand. I confess to being a bit intimidated by my own ignorance of things so important to you, Joan. You'll need patience to help me try to catch up.

This has to be brief. I'm proofing 18 pages of *The Osprey*, our wild steelhead newsletter, and must get it done before bed—a last-minute chore that I forgot about in the excitement of today.

I'm running out of adjectives about the way I feel about you, my Beautiful. It is just about impossible to come close to describing how you have changed my outlook on life. I just want to live for you, however feeble the attempts may have to be!!

You are so precious and special to me. Do sleep well. I intend to. I love you beyond words. John

Sent 10:30 p.m., 6-2
John, You are so good and I feel bad that I didn't get a "Good Night" message to you after that lovely afternoon. My excuse is that although I fully intended to check for a word from you before 8:30 and then send you a bedtime "I love You," I fell asleep in front of the TV until too late. Maybe if I would go to bed earlier and get in 7 or 8 hours a night that wouldn't happen.

Yes, that CV is a copy you can have. Don't feel bad about not understanding everything. How can you? I am just trying to share my life with you so you will understand me better. I am trying to learn as much as I can about *your* life and what goes on inside your head. There is no doubt that there is a strong connection of shared likes and opinions, and a history of friendship and respect for each other, but we are already way beyond that. WE are filling in the gaps, maybe learning why we love each other so. I love learning about you, and I'll probably need lots of explanation. Feel free to ask *me* anything, I'll do my best to clarify.

I love being in your arms. I wish I were there right now, but this afternoon's memory is sweet and will carry me till Monday.

This was an enchanted day. Thank you for making me feel so cherished.

ILY,

Joan

6-3, morning
Hi,

Unbeknownst to you, my Precious, I've been sweating just a tad about yesterday because there were ten eyewitnesses, all friends of ours, to the fact that I was *not* at the luncheon. None of them, that I know of, know how to reach me because I have not given out my home phone number while I'm on this special assignment. But you never know, what with computer-ready phone books.

Yes, you should get more rest. I don't care when, just get it! I don't expect a good night from you every evening, I know what's in your heart. That's really all that matters.

Gotta go for now.

Endless love,

John

2:40 pm, 6-3
Hi again,

I hope that "order" about getting rest didn't come across as being harsh, I didn't mean it that way, rather to encourage you to take care of yourself. You have someone else who is concerned about *you* now, don't forget. Have I "earned" my right to be concerned about you???

I'm still on a high from yesterday afternoon, the most delicious sandwich I ever ate, the most incredible dining partner, the most idyllic surroundings and the most Beautiful Person I have ever known. Maybe this whole arrangement was *designed* to make me wait such a long time, like 50+ years!

Bally was great this morning, I did all "my" machines, a little more than last time, small-steps building. I'm reminded I didn't cough in your presence, but coughed a lot once I got back to my pad. Hmmmm. Cough seems better today, although it may be back as the evening approaches. If it does I'll get an appointment with the doc as this has been lingering long enough.

Beloved, Beautiful Joan. What a joy you are to me, I love you so.

Must go, more when I can.

John

8:30 p.m., 6-3
Oh John, when I saw that title on the Inbox, I imagined all manner of scary things. I am so glad you are not in the phone book. It had crossed my mind that someone might try to call you, wondering why you weren't at the I-Hop. We walk a tight rope, don't we? I guess you are used to that sort of thing, but I wonder what will happen if you are found out. Would it mess up your assignment here, could your Boss make it right?

I just got your second message of the day. Sweet talk will get you anywhere; and yes, you have earned the right to be concerned about me, as I think I have about you. Please take note of the paragraph above. So far you have never said anything to me that has seemed harsh in any way. I remember that brief time in the convertible when you put your hand over mine and told me you wanted to help me. I felt then that you were sincere. I know it now, for sure.

About the cough. It could be an allergy, do have it checked if it keeps up. Please.

Tonight I am going to take Libby to the Women's University Club for the Seafood Buffet. She is a real fan of any kind of seafood. I am driving and picking up my friends Don and Marcia Johnson to go with us. They are not related to me except that Marcia and I think we might have some common relatives back a few generations. Her maiden name was Chandler which was my Dad's middle name from a family surname on his mother's side. So she and I both have "Walkers" in our backgrounds. That was my grandmother's maiden name and there are a slew of Revolutionary War Walkers buried in the cemetery in Brattleboro, Vermont. I've been there. My grandmother was a DAR. I could be too, but won't because they won't accept adopted daughters (Libby). Now aren't you delighted to have that bit of information about me? Now you can tell me about *your* heritage. What nationality is your surname? Mine, of course is German. You, no doubt, know that.

Enough for now. If I'm not too tired, I will send you a written goodnight kiss. If it doesn't happen forgive me because I'll be taking your advice and getting some rest.

Love you more and more,
Joan

7:50 p.m., 6-3
My surname is German, too. It is also Dutch, my dad's side nationality. He was 100 percent Dutch, my mom 100 Swede. Another connection. What was your mom?

Hey, I notice now I'm on page 101 of my running (protected) document of all our e-mails and notes. Hope to bring it with me to the ocean if I can get my laptop to work properly. We can review it and watch our love grow, together, on the record!!

Gotta go, again. You should be getting home by now? Rest well, my love. Twenty-four hours away is too much. ILY
John

9 p.m., 6-3
John, I thought maybe I would have a chance to say "Goodnight," it's only 9:10 or so. I was wondering if your name might be German, too, but I don't know why. Nice to know it is. I've never been heavily into genealogy, but some of my relatives have been, so I have some parts of my family tree sorted out for me.

I got everyone safely home after two glasses of wine . . . lots of seafood, dessert and coffee. Several people were drinking Manhattans. You set a very good example which I obviously didn't follow. Don't scold.

I'll bet you are in bed now, if not sleep tight and dream something nice with me a part of it. Otherwise, Good Morning. Either way, hugs and kisses. Love you.

Joan

PS
The card is great, and in a yellow envelope too. What a nice surprise. You do such happy things for me. Thank you.

Check List

dictionary
bibles (hers, *The* Message; yours)
two lawn chairs
camp stool
seat pad purple
back pack

bird feeder, seed and "hook" ?
kite bag, loaded
?brief case w/ citations, Dean photo, mom/dad, medals ??
laptop
cell phone
cell phone charger
flash drive, recently updated
coffee and coffee kit
sleeping bag
pillow
toilet kit w/ meds, etc.
pads (4)
mouth wash
black beach shoes
Hiking boots II
jeans
towels small
sun glasses
sox, heavy & street
undies, 4 pr top/bottom
jammies
bathrobe
beach pants
fleece suit
walking shorts
summer & winter shirts (2 ea)
khaki slacks
blue wind breaker
binoculars
satellite Rx
ice chest w/ two blocks ice
Food:
milk, cereal, v-8, grapefruit juice (get at OS?), bananas, bread,
Stoly (she will have), sandwich makings for the road, NZ cheese,
salteens, hummus

sent 9:20 a.m., 6-4
Good morning, Sunshine!

I've been up and running since 0500, and I had two very welcome greetings from my Mercer Island friend. But I think MSN may have cheated you, again, as I checked about 9:45 last night and found nothing there, even though your first message was "time stamped" 8:30 p.m. You said it was after 9 so something's wrong, I suspect MSN overload.

Sounds like a great evening. I, too, love seafood, so long as it's not spicy-hot! No, Jo-an, you will not teach me to enjoy Thai cooking. You have to allow for my age, remember.

My, how I miss you. What about a little Tiffany on Monday and I wear my Superman suit. Or is it too scratchy *for you*??? Again, your call, My Precious.

ILY, Me

7:30 p.m., 6-4

John, I think I have been missing you all day. I NEED you in my life constantly. Unbelievable that I would feel that a few months ago, but whatever it is that has happened to me has changed everything.

I spent most of the day with Libby, and found that I was resenting her presence, only because I wanted free access to e-mail and you.

Now I am determined that you will receive this before you go to bed. I am sorry about last night and MSN's inability to get my messages to you. I'm hoping to do better now.

Libby wanted to come today instead of Sunday because she is going to Port Angeles tomorrow for a birthday party. That was fine. She did laundry. We went to Costco to get my Meds, and Copper River Salmon. Then we worked in the yard and she gave me a lot of help with planting and weeding etc. She carried the heavy stuff up to the garage for me. I am afraid of that chore, ever since the eye stroke that happened when I did that last year. She wanted me to cook dinner here. I did. We were both exhausted by our gardening efforts, but she rested while I cooked, set the table etc. Isn't it typical that kids revert to Mom being Mom and doing it all when they come home? Maybe guys don't notice that, but every woman I know does. I gave her half of the uncooked small whole salmon I bought to take home.

I feel better now that I have vented a little. If I hadn't felt I was missing out on connecting with you, it wouldn't have bothered me so much. It didn't really matter because we weren't connecting anyway except in my hopes. You were on my mind and in my heart all day.

We can have a Tiffany Monday. I will be prepared. I am also wondering if you will have eaten before you come. If it is more convenient, I could make a pot of soup and have it ready at 7:00 for a quick simple meal, or I will eat early and wait eagerly for your arrival. Hair down???

I long for the sweet peace of being wrapped in your arms.

I love you. Thank you for loving me.

Joan

9:31 p.m., 6-4
What a beautiful day you have described for me and I am honored by your frankness of expression about your feelings. Amazing how much the same we feel about each other, you say it much better than I. Thank you, my Sunshine, for sharing your very satisfying day with me. Yes, I do understand how moms get leaned on, dads, too, I've learned, but not nearly so much.
Love you, love you, John

Early afternoon 6-5
John, I just got home from church. It is very late because we had a Congregational Lunch after, then a special program with the

new organ. First thing I did was to check phone messages. I am *so* looking forward to tomorrow.

This morning before leaving for Choir Practice, I checked my e-mail and was so delighted by the message you sent last night that it brought tears to my eyes. Those were tears of joy.

Today was Communion Sunday. You Lutherans probably have it weekly, but we do only on first Sundays and special occasions. You probably know that too. I would be happy with it every Sunday. It is my favorite service.

Our Anthem went well, in spite of the fact that we had to sing, as well, during communion. That was a complete surprise. We quickly learned a hymn that no one had ever heard before, and still managed the difficult, "How Lovely is Thy Dwelling Place," as our major presentation.

I am still in my church clothes. Think I'll go out in my garden and keep at it, it needs lots of work. I'll wait for your next e-mail, but it was good that you phoned. The sound of your voice always helps me.

I love you and want/need you near me,

Joan

Evening, 6-5
Hi,

Good news: I've arranged my team's work schedule so I should have no trouble getting out of here in time to enjoy that special soup of yours! Can hardly wait. I love you so, Joan.

8:12 p.m., 6-5
John, I've been out in my garden, again, I want it to look at least half-way decent when you come tomorrow.

So far June 14, 20, and 21 are good. It is a big B.A.M. week (Bellevue Arts Museum) because of many parties. I'll be going to a fancy one on the 15th, and two on Friday the 17th. The Grand Opening is on Saturday the 18th.

You should be proud of me. The past two nights I have been in bed by eleven. Still woke up early but lay quietly awake thinking of you and remembering the pleasures of being with you.

I have been thinking of your Dutch-Swedish heritage. Libby is Swedish, but that doesn't seem at all interesting to her. No wonder you are a blue-eyed blond. I do like your very clear blue eyes. Have you been to Holland? I loved Amsterdam in spite of its liberal agenda.

More questions to answer. What are your parents' first names? Where did they grow up? Where did they go to college? I figure your mom was a college student too, because you were surprised that my mom was not. She also insisted that you marry a college graduate? Did you know your grandparents? How, When, Where? How did your mom and dad get together and why? I'll bet you were doted on by your parents and every one else in the larger family. You were so cute and bright. I remember that. And, I'll bet that you were one of the boys I chased and kissed in those primary grade years. My sister teases me about that. I must have been a naughty little girl.

John, I have a million questions about you. I guess I want to know everything there is to know. I have been thinking today about all the things I admire about you. First, I suppose is the fact that we connect on so many levels. But I applaud the fact that you have given your life to serving your country, you are using your strong mental abilities to do good in our world, you love Jesus and try to live your life to God's will. You are strong, yet gentle and kind. You can be in charge and people rely on you. You have humor. You are mannerly and well behaved. You have the ability to make things happen. That's only a start, my dear, I am constantly impressed and grateful that you find me worthy of your love. You certainly are worthy of mine.

minutes later

John, What happened? I'm sitting here for far too long writing to you. I guess that is better for me than eating or sleeping. I should be doing both. Hope you got my long message and that everything is OK. I will go eat now, then check again. Still loving you, Joan

9 p.m., 6-5
My Precious One,

I'm pretty sure that my work schedule will allow you plenty of leeway for your BAM functions. It's not essential that I'm there for those, even though I would really want to be. Main thing is that *you* are there.

I loved Amsterdam, was there for two days, but don't really remember that much about the details, a boat cruise on a canal and walks among the windmills. Yes, their politics and social ideas are terrible.

If I ever need to apply for a job and want a reference, I know where to turn!! You're too kind (prejudiced?). But I *do* like to get things done and hate to be at the mercy of people who only talk about things but rarely act effectively. Intelligence officers, at least the ops guys among us, have to be that way, we don't get many chances to succeed.

My maternal grandmother lived with us in '35, for one year (first grade). She was born in '65, the year Lincoln was shot, I believe. Her husband, my grandfather, died shortly after my mom was born, so I never knew him, of course. On my dad's side I knew both my grandparents, they died while I was in high school, very nice people.

My mom's mom was a stickler on college education, she put all five of her kids through four-year degree programs, her eldest went to med school but died in the '20's flu epidemic shortly after interning at Cook County in Chicago. (That's Kitty's father.) Very strong people, all of these, solid in their faith and very hard workers. One of my mom's brothers sang in the Hollywood Presbyterian choir for many years, and in their quartet as the bass, he taught music in the LA school system. His son, my cousin Jon, went on to be the provost at Eastman School of Music, a huge job.

So much love, so much to say, so much to share. Tomorrow we can do it face to face!!!

John

John spends the next evening, Monday, with Joan, in her home.

Morning 6-7

John, So much to think about after last evening.

There is no doubt in my mind that you and I have a great affinity for each other. When we talk, even on the phone, we laugh a lot and have fun just connecting. Isn't that wonderful? It makes me feel so happy. That makes me feel that we really do belong together. Too bad we missed out so many years along the way, but I am so glad we have it now. I cannot even begin to express the joy you have brought into my life.

I like it when you share things with me about what is going on in your church and your feelings about Jesus. I think you will help me to increase my faith which is already really strong. Cliff was a believer, but less able to express himself publicly than I. When we needed to pray, he wanted me to do it. We didn't do grace before meals except when the kids were small, and they did it. But I always feel the need at family gatherings, and I was always the one who would pray. You make me feel that all of this is part of my life. I love it when we pray together. You are increasing my faith and that is a true blessing. I thank God for you several times each day, and, of course, I pray for you, and I am secure in the belief that you pray for me.

I am going out to my garden, again. I feel so elated about yesterday. Now I long even more for those times we can be together.
Joan

Sent 7 p.m., 6-7
My dearest Joan,

We were so wrapped up in each other last night, I never did quite say what I had written earlier, some how I apparently forgot to push the "Send" button.

Those beautiful words you wrote make me feel kind of inadequate, My Precious. I think so highly of you—and have for so long—that I really wonder if I'm worthy of your adoration, so strongly you express it. Don't get me wrong, I love your words and your beauty (your *soul*, really) which I can see as clearly as though I were still with you in your family room. Yes, I pray many times daily for you, for your safety, health, your peace of mind.

Good night and sweet dreams!!

John

10 p.m., 6-7 "You understand"
John, I'm here right now to try to catch you before you go to sleep. Thank you for my goodnight message. It means a lot to me. If I didn't trust you so, I would never have the courage to be so open about the way I feel.

May God keep you safe, make you strong again and keep you well. May He bless our love and let us share it abundantly. I am so thankful for you. You have changed my life and filled me with

a joy I wish I could share with the world. Goodnight my Dearest.
I love you so.

Joan

8 p.m., 6-7
Joan: If you've checked your answering machine, you'll hear
a few giggles, although it's not funny to miss connecting.
I've actually had a crummy day, beginning when I learned of
some missed deadlines by one of my writers. This hardly ever
happens and the guy has been ill, he just missed the dates!
But as the chief of this unit, it's my responsibility. Long stories,
both, but right now I'm not a happy camper. These are some of
my warts showing. I could cope, with more equanimity, if you
were close by.

Maybe I'm spoiled but I resent our not being able to see and
hold each other whenever we want!! Connections, holding,
soothing, caressing, loving, smiling, eyes in eyes, lips on lips,
what a wonderful memory.
Giddy with love for you,
John

Hi John,
11 a.m., 6-8
I just sat down at the computer to start writing minutes for my
guild. Just needed to connect for a moment. I was happy to get
to talk to you this morning. It was the best part of my day. It has
been a day of paying bills and corporation taxes. That boggles my
no-math brain. I'll get back to you later, MY Darling.

9:30 p.m.
"I am here for you"
Dear Giddy, I just turned on my computer a few minutes ago to
talk to you, but your message made me turn it off so I could go
listen to your phone calls. At least you were laughing your way
through the problems. I laughed with you but also suffered for
you. I'm sorry I was unavailable. I turned the computer on, sent

you that brief little message, then started to concentrate on my minutes. That's why you couldn't reach me by phone. I stayed on the Internet. That is another reason to abandon the dial-up and change to Comcast. It is nice to be needed, and I'm sorry I couldn't help.

I'll take a few of your warts! Too much perfection is hard to cope with. Wish I could kiss away the hurts. I, too, long for the next time we're together, when we can take up where we left off. The emotional connections are always there, but those lovely physical connections are in my thoughts all the time we are separated. How I do miss them. I love you, John and hope tomorrow is a better day.

Joan

6:45 a.m. 6-8
"Better?""
John, I know you probably didn't get last night's e-mail till this morning. I'm still concerned about your bad day yesterday. It just seems important to touch base early. I'll be heading off for exercise at nine, and following that with some errands. I should be home somewhere between noon and one if you get a chance to call.

In the meantime, I'll be praying for a better day today, and sending lots of love your way. Wish I could hold you tight right now. Joan

6 p.m., 6-8
John,

I hate being so far away and separated. Even a few moments to cling to each other would help ease the tension. You must know that my whole concentration is devoted to you right now, my thoughts, my prayers and my love. *We* are meant to be. It is such a strong feeling. I can't make it go away, and I don't want to.

You are enveloped in my love, I hope you can feel it.

Now I'd better go, until sometime tomorrow.

ILY, Joan

6-9
Hi,

I'm really too old for this sort of thing, do you know that??!! Arnie Palmer is our age and his nerves went out about three years ago but his problem was that little white ball, not a government bureaucracy, so far as I know.

I'm running on Jo-an-energy, love tonic, super-charged sweet nectar. I am zany kooky dingy off my rocker in love with this unbelievably lovely woman who is dingy enough to love me back! Crazy with love, I think they call this.

I'm editing Romans 5: 1-8 as I type this, reading it Sunday; it has meaning for both of us, down at the very human (sinner) level. See what your Message has to say.

Here's how my reading will go: St. Paul's remarkable statement about the presence of God's love in our hearts with a hope that never disappoints—all owing to Christ's death for each of us undeserving sinners. From the 5th chapter of his letter to the church at Rome.

"Since we are justified through faith, we have peace with God through our Lord Jesus Christ, 2through whom we have obtained access to this grace in which we stand. And we boast in our hope sharing the glory of God. 3And not only that, but we also boast in our sufferings, knowing that suffering produces endurance; 4and endurance produces character; and character produces hope. 5And hope does not disappoint us, because God's love has been poured into our hearts through the Holy Spirit that has been given to us.

"For while we were still weak, at the right time Christ died for the ungodly. 7Indeed, rarely will anyone die for a righteous person, though perhaps for a good person someone might actually dare to die. 8But God proves his love for us in that while we still were sinners, Christ died for us."

Sorry, but that brings tears, which I will control at the lectern. You see, my Precious, I'm convinced that He *wants* us to love each other and have a happiness in that love that could never exist without it. That's what just a few months of your presence in my life has come to mean. I couldn't be more sincere about that.

I should close for now.

ILY John

7:21p.m., 6-9
I've got it too, John, CRAZY in love with you. I need you so much that I am going nuts waiting for our next chance to be together. I laughed out loud with pleasure all through your second paragraph. Happy laughter because you are making me feel so special to you. I thank God for that. I thank you too, for loving me and making me feel so loved.

I can't imagine you at *top* energy. Hours on end with your writers and Washington, doing Bible Study every week, reading during Sunday Service, *and* keeping me happy, seems to me like it takes an enormous amount of energy. I think you are an amazing person. Take care. Give yourself time to recover. Take those naps. You are a force for good in this world, and I am honored that you care for me. It will really be awesome when you fully recover. I can hardly wait for that experience.

I, too, feel close to tears reading Paul's message. John, you are so wise and you are helping me to learn and appreciate things that the Bible says which add to my knowledge and my faith. I am glad for your belief because it enforces and enriches mine. That is a special blessing of our love.

Today I was at home most of the time. I worked hard finishing and mailing those minutes I had to get to my guild. Then I put in time in my yard because I have invited my old Arboretum Unit to lunch. For many years long ago I belonged to this group which was a source of information about gardening. We met, had speakers, and learned a lot. Once a year we went to help weed the Arboretum, and probably gave them money through our dues. We called ourselves the "Late Bloomers." Now we get together only once a year for lunch. This year is my turn. I set a date for lunch. Now I have this huge incentive to really get my yard in order, so they don't think I have become a terrible gardener. I have been working some every day. You saw how overgrown every thing is. Today I weeded, trimmed, and pulled out overgrown ivy. There is still lots to do. Making them lunch is no problem, taking care of my garden is.

I think you and I are both people who enjoy being involved and making things happen. We both work hard and like the feeling. That helps connect us. But oh, My Darling, I need more connection. I am missing you so much that I ache. I pray that we will be together soon.

Thank you for your note today. It has warmed my heart, made me feel very loved and very happy. I am helplessly in love with you.

Joan

10 p.m., 6-9
You read me very well, Dear Lady, and it *is* almost spooky how we "fit."

ILY John

Sent 6:49, a.m.
The Message: Romans 5: "By entering through faith into what God has always wanted to do for us—set us right with Him, make us fit for Him—we have it altogether with God because of our Master Jesus. And that's not all: We throw open our doors to God

and discover at the same moment that He has already thrown open His door to us. We find ourselves standing where we always hoped we might stand—out in the wide open spaces of God's grace and glory, standing tall and shouting our praise.

"There's more to come: We continue to shout our praise even when we're hemmed in with troubles, because we know how troubles can develop passionate patience in us, and how that patience in turn forges the tempered steel of virtue, keeping us alert for whatever God will do next. In alert expectancy such as this, we're never left feeling shortchanged. Quite the contrary— we can't round up enough containers to hold everything God generously pours into our lives through the Holy Spirit.

"Christ arrives right on time to make this happen. He didn't and doesn't wait for us to get ready. He presented himself for this sacrificial death when we were far too weak and rebellious to do anything to get ourselves ready. And even if we hadn't been so weak, we wouldn't have known what to do anyway. We can understand someone dying for a person worth dying for, and we can understand how someone good and noble could inspire us to selfless sacrifice. But God put his love on the line for us by offering his Son in sacrificial death while we were of no use whatever to him."

I typed most of this last night. Thought I'd give it to you for comparison. Good Morning. Have a peaceful day.

ILY, Joan

8:15 a.m., 6-10
Good morning to you, too!

My, I could hardly believe the time stamp: 6:49 a.m. That's a lot of typing, too, and I do appreciate your doing that for me. In any language, Paul has it right for all of us.

Your account of your day and the "Late Bloomers" fascinates me, Joan. I want to hear more about this. You're a never-ending source of fascinating personal history, yet I'm less and less surprised to hear all these things.

Again, I'm very short on time and have to run. Sorry, I want to write and write and write.

Madly (still—always) in love with you,

John

6:45 p.m., 6-10
Hi,

It's about 4:30 now and my gang is doing final edits on some difficult draft tracts on the Somali pirates situation, something the world pays little attention to, I think, eventually, at our peril.

I never hear you complain, by the way, and can't imagine that your life never has had any bumps along the way, with all the people and situations you deal with. I hope you feel just as free to "air it out" with me as I do with you!! My shoulders are pretty broad and I cherish having your head on them, even with a few frowns and tears now and then.

At my church's luncheon, by the way, I was in charge of the devotions—as I am each month—and this time I composed one myself. I usually get them off the Internet and then edit away to suit myself and the occasion. But this time I wanted to put Jesus at each table, as the Honored Guest, as this was a kind of special "feast," and so I did that. I'll share it with you sometime.

By now, 6:45, it's about time to leave the office and I'll send this and hope to write more before bed. If not, know that I'm thinking about you constantly, in prayer and every other way. I love you so.

John

6p.m., 6-10
Hi John, I just sent you a brief message cuz I couldn't get the attachment to work for me. I'm hoping that it is something about the Bellevue Arts Museum. There was a really good story in the King County Journal this morning which I cut out to show you. I am excited about the museum's opening because I really believe it will be well accepted.

Tonight I have been invited to dinner at the home of friends, so I probably won't be home in time to get a Goodnight e-mail off to you. This may have to do.

I've been groggy and achy today. Maybe the intensive yard work is catching up. I even took a nap and really conked. I didn't get to bed very early last night, but I got up for my exercise class and managed that OK. I'm really missing you, and that doesn't help. I count the days till Tuesday.

It tickles me that you respond as you do to my "history." I'm surprised that you are intrigued by the Late Bloomers. It did help me with gardening skills. One thing I am proud of having done was through my Children's Orthopedic Hospital Guild. Now it is referred to as Children's Hospital. I joined it when I first moved to Mercer Island in the early 50's. Their efforts to help the hospital were to place mobiles in every child's room, to make them, and place them according to sex of child, season, age, etc. They were made of heavy paper and painted, strung so they turned properly, and changed every month. For twelve years I designed every one. They each had a theme. We worked one day a week, most of the time in my home, cutting and painting and putting together. We would make several of each design and had big supplies of them. A crew would go to the hospital to hang them. Sometimes I helped with that too. We climbed ladders to hang them over the beds where the kids could watch them. Sometimes we had to don sterile outfits before entering the room of a burn victim, etc. Everyone in the guild was 10 years older than I. The guild is emeritus now, but I think we did a lot of good with those mobiles. Now, it seems very long ago.

As always, you have been in my thoughts, and in my heart most of the day. I have this deep longing that won't go away until we are together. I feel better when I am either writing to you or reading your words to me, the rest of the time I ache. What a deal! YOU MAKE ME SO HAPPY, but sometimes I feel bad because it has been too long. I can hardly wait to see you. And by the way, shall I fix something to eat for Tuesday? It seems logical, just eat fast because there are more important things to do. Still dinner by candle light might not be bad.

I love you John,

Joan

Joan,

It's a story about art museums around the country and how they're changing their "approach" to attract more visitors and supporters. And, stupid of me, the password is "our" password: jjinlove. I'll bet it works!!

I know you'll enjoy your evening with friends, it is so neat that you are asked out to share with people you enjoy. I know you are loved by so many, you're just that kind of Lady.

If you see this before bed, know that my love burns all night, for you, you, you.

John

11 p.m., 6-10
You are, I hope, sound asleep and dreaming of me. I just got home and need a little quiet time to ease me into sleep. What better thing than to sit here thinking of you.

I loved discovering that the "Password" is "Ours." jjinlove worked beautifully. What fun. It was an interesting article. My college history came to me entirely through History of Art,

History of Sculpture, etc. I believe art definitely expresses history, and of course, wherever I have traveled I have headed for Art Museums. I like all kinds of museums but art comes first. I want to expose you to the joys of art. More people spend time and money investigating cultural things than ball games, etc. That always surprises me, but it is true. You can teach me about the things you love and I will be glad to share those things with you. You have already taught me a lot and I love learning and sharing your interests. You will get a good dose of mine as well. I am sure.

My evening was very interesting. The couple who invited me is made up of the husband of my "best friend," who got caught in that compromising situation I told you about, and left her marriage to be with her lover, and the second, the wife of this man. She is now my regular bridge partner for the St. Monica's tournament, and a good friend. Also included were the guy's daughter and her husband. I have known them both for years. That is probably too complex and you couldn't care less, but it was casual and comfortable. The best part of the evening was this: They have a clear western view overlooking the lake, the city, and the floating bridge. To the left of the dining table area windows is a tall fir tree. All during dinner, we watched two eagles building a nest. They kept carrying huge branches up to the branch second from the top of the fir, and by the time we finished dinner, the female was settled into the nest. They will be able to watch an eagle family grow this summer. What a blessing. I see lots of eagles from my house, but never a nest. Sometimes I have seen young ones learning to fly, but this was really special. They got out a book and we read about the nesting habits of eagles, how they mate for life and take turns caring for the young etc. It was great entertainment.

Sunday afternoon I will be going to the Pops Symphony with other friends. I do like regular symphony too. I know you do. My dad always put on classical music in the evenings at home. I am not all smooth jazz, Frank Sinatra, Dean Martin, Glen Miller, but you probably know more about the classics than I. I *do* recognize Beethoven's Fifth.

Time to settle down. I love being loved by you, John. I love you back, at least as much as you love me. I just wish there were more chances to show it. Soon???? *I live for the moment.*

4:15 p.m., 6-11
Well, now I'm envious and you've just made yourself a date with me for sometime in February '06 when we will stroll, hand in hand, down a very comfortable rails-to-trails path along the Carbon River (near Orting) and watch a dozen or more mature Bald Eagles fishing for salmon. (If I scope it out properly ahead of time, that is.)

Another connection? Yes, indeed. I'm enthralled by those birds, have watched them along the Skagit River for years (while fly fishing for steelhead), especially their courtship "death spirals." And in Canada once I saw them working on a nest as big as a Volkswagen Beetle, many years old as they just add branches to them year by year. I spotted two of them just last week, soaring upward in a powerful thermal between my pad and Lake Sammamish. Still, they're not so plentiful as to be common and every sighting is a thrill, as you were reminded last evening. So thanks a ton for sharing that with me: You are *so special* to do that! Just another of a zillion reasons for loving you so.

It's a long day, today, without you, My Most Precious Person. But it's Paul in spades: suffering produces endurance, endurance patience, etc. It is beyond me how your image sustains me every waking moment. You truly are my Goddess, not so long ago a kind of vague image, now a most powerful reality.

I will think about and pray for you in church tomorrow, Joan, as I know you will for me. Sleep well, My Beauty, rest in God's arms. ILY, John

5 p.m., 6-11
Just occurred to me: Do you have on MI something called "Relay for Life"? It used to be a cancer celebration thing in Sumner and a whole bunch of people showed up in August and filled Spartan Stadium, the survivors walked around the track, everybody applauds them, many groups show up with booths/tents to display their wares/services, collect money, all for the ACS. I'll be a two-time survivor when they do it again in August, just got a reminder card in the mail. You could be a three-timer. Maybe someday we can walk together (or be wheeled, say 15 years from now) around the track together. Now that would be cool!!

5:40, 6-11
I accept. We can celebrate my birthday—February 1, have I told you?—watching eagles on the Carbon River. I'm delighted about all your connections with those eagles. Thank you for sharing your experiences with me. I have seen one of those giant eagle nests in the Museum in Victoria, B.C. It amazed me. Isn't it wonderful that you and I are thrilled by many of the same things? I feel entwined with you. I wish I *were* right now.

I have spent time today double deleting e-mails that I don't need to keep, like one liners, edits, etc. Then I have been double checking things that go or have now gone into my safe file. Thank you for that. I have so much to check and it takes hours but I want to keep forever your precious words to me. You sure do know how to talk to me. Wow! There are so many things that are keepers, treasures to me.

I've been home alone all day with nothing to divert my thoughts of you. It seemed like a long time before I heard from you, but I kept telling myself not to worry. You sent me three e-mails yesterday, but I was so happy to get the newest three a while ago. I was glad for Kitty's message and impressed with what the judge said. Isn't it sad that the general public doesn't have access to these things.

The Cancer walks occur around here too, but not on Mercer Island. I haven't participated, but I do try to do a little personal help for people I know who have cancer. There are a lot. I have kept a list of personal women friends who have had cancer. It is way over thirty. Happily most are survivors. That may be because they have been faithful in being checked and so were caught early. One very dear and close friend died from it. I'll count on US rolling along in our wheelchairs or maybe on roller skates 15 years from now as happy and together survivors.

Time to get my dinner. You may not hear from me till late tomorrow. If not, know that I am thinking about you and loving you. It is a permanent state of mind, My Darling.

Joan

7:30 p.m., 6-12
Hi,
Hey, I think I can arrange my work load so we can be together (your place, of course) on Tuesday. Soup/bread OK with you? Kind of a "Lenten" menu which we have at our church each week during that season. Besides, I need some practice eating soup with a Real Lady who will be patient with me at her own table, less so in a fancy restaurant. (Two warts, here: Hot soup can make my nose run a bit, and I tend to eat it too fast, especially when it's very good as I know yours will be. Don't say you weren't warned!)

Love you always, John

8:30 p.m., 6-12
Hey, how many in your congregation do that "light on the lips kisses"?, in those passing-the-peace situations? Presbyterians are much more reserved than that. I'm afraid if I came to your church, I would embarrass the whole congregation if I were standing close to you. But it sounds like fun to me.

Thank you for the phone message. Of course, the minute I got home late this afternoon, I checked the e-mail. You knew I would wonder, and gave me the peace of the phone message. That kind of understanding is so important to me. You never fail. Thank you for that.

I had a wonderful day. No choir today for church, but we will sing next Sunday before stopping completely for summer. This was the Sunday when the graduating High School Students did the complete service. Our youth ministry is awesome. The pastor who leads it is HIV Positive and married to a beautiful young woman who just received her doctorate degree in religion—with honors. The kids in this program are inspiring, and the whole service filled everyone with God's love. You were there with me through the whole thing. I could feel it.

The Pops Symphony, which began at 2:00 pm, was equally fabulous. It put me on a high for the entire afternoon. I thought about you through all the love songs and wanted you beside me holding my hand. They were mostly love songs.

I have already started the soup we will have on Tuesday. Don't worry about anything. I will have a big box of Kleenex nearby. This will be the easiest do-ahead meal we can have. I am so excited and have finally allowed myself to count on it, after the past frustrations. If you can be here earlier I will be overjoyed. I am living in a world that is so different from anything I ever expected to be a part of my life, yet it is a world I cannot give up because of my feelings for you. They are so strong, John, and influencing all of my decisions, good or bad. I can't help it.

Our being together is the most important thing to me. It is hard to come by, yet the most fulfilling thing I can think of. I am counting the hours now instead of the days. If I weren't so secure in your love, *I wouldn't be comfortable telling you these things.*

Goodnight my love, Sweet Dreams filled with the hope that we will be in each other's arms soon. Thank God. I can hardly wait. I love you.

Joan

9 p.m., 6-13, after phone call earlier
Hi,

After that wonderful phone conversation, I've been reviewing our e-mail love notes and I became mesmerized with what a wonderful progression it is for me to see you "warm" to our relationship. April 30 was the turn, for me, when you said it on the phone, "I love you, too." And look at us six weeks later!

Here's what I had started to write earlier today, about Passing the Peace in our Lutheran Church.

The kissing is for spouses only and not many of them do it. After the initial "peck" they go around shaking hands and hugging people, passing the peace as you apparently know it too. They're aren't many couples who kiss, and we bachelors just watch and smile!

You caused me some pause, my Most Precious, when you used the word Honeymoon this evening. We've both been avoiding the "M" word, too, as in marriage, although I would never expect you to bring it up first, but I'm sure we've both thought about it. I don't want to even get near this topic tomorrow but I hope you'll agree we should talk about it *extensively* while we're on the beach. My thinking has progressed a lot in the past couple of weeks, maybe yours has too, and we owe it to each other to share as best we can. I need more time to sort it out and to think about how things are going at the office and with my contract and I really do want to be absolutely certain that you're not in love with a mirage. Your notes to me are so overwhelmingly beautiful and uplifting—no one has ever come close to this kind of appreciation of me, believe me—it's hard to believe I'm really that deserving. And to disappoint you would absolutely kill me. So let's be as careful and honest about this as we can, and I know we will. Look for the warts, Joan, you really should.

I hope I haven't caused you to wait too long for this, Joan. It's an important message, deep from my heart.

Sleep with smiles for me, my Beauty. I love you so. John

9:20 p.m., 6-13
Hi, again,

Breathless for tomorrow.
ILY, John

8:15 p.m., 6-13
John, I know you will send me some kind of message tonight, but I want to be sure you know about my day tomorrow. I will be leaving my house about 10:15 to play bridge at the other end of the Island. I should be home a little after three. You said maybe you could come earlier than we had hoped. Let me know. I will try to be here whenever you can get here.

I am a little worried about the soup I made. I love it, but it is a little bit spicy hot. I don't want to do you in. I can always make a pot of Pablum. Just kidding, not being mean. I can come up with something simpler and quick. I do not want to hurt you in any way.

If you call after Bible Study, I should still be here. I will expect some message tonight. Loved our conversation earlier. Love you. Joan

Reply about 9:30 p.m., 6-13
Hey, leave that soup alone!! I want to learn what you call "a little" spicy-hot!!!

Since we're dining tomorrow, you can read my devotion for our seniors' barbeque last Friday. Not precisely appropriate, but close. MSWord attachment.

'Nite. ILY sooooooo much.
John

11:40 a.m., 6-14
Hi,
I got home this morning, not long after we talked, to a leaking hot water heater which for a few moments threatened to scrub our date today. But as it lucked out the plumber will be here first thing in the morning, just right, and I'll have all the hot water I need.

The "bad news" is that I'll be stuck here until just before five. I see the dentist (routine cleaning) at 1:30 so I'll be Ipana White (remember that?) for you! Less that six hours to go!! ILY John

After 3.5 hr visit evening 6-14.

About 9:40 a.m., 6-15
Good Morning,

I had a number of things on my "agenda" to talk about last night, Sweetheart, but obviously got caught up in the thrill of just being with you, so my memory kind of blanked out. But one item we probably should think about is how/when I get into your world back in MI/Bellevue after we come back from the beach. I guess church is out on the 3rd but what about the latter part of Sunday? And the Fourth? And do we want to come back after two nights or three? (We have reservations for three but don't have to use the 3rd night.) I think I know the answer to this but maybe we should just wait and see. Whatever day we come back, I'll need most of that afternoon to get you home, then park the motor home at my place and clean it up a bit before putting it back in storage. I'll spend the night of the Fourth at my pad although it might be fun to watch fireworks together somewhere near your home if that's possible, then I scoot home, pack for Montana and take off morning of the 5th, stopping at your place, spend the day/night with you and then head for Montana *very* early morning of the 6th, without coming back home. Hope that all makes sense.

Every time we get together, my Most Precious, we seem to reach new highs, at least that's what I felt last evening. I suppose this can't go on forever, ever upward, but I'm eager to find out. You were absolutely stunning in that outfit, Joan, I'll never forget it, nor your "simple" meal, just so tastefully done, everything just right. (Don't expect such perfection in the motor home, it isn't possible!!)

I'd better run now, the plumber and his near-$700 bill is coming any moment.

I love you so, my Sunshine.

John

6-15, a.m. Note (not sent to Joan but part of our e-mail collection)
Further to your being with Joan, evening 6-14: As you drove into her driveway and saw her there in the doorway with that world-class smile that she uses so easily, your knees nearly buckled before you opened the car door. She had on an outfit that would stop trains, so classy and cute and exquisite all at once and her silver hair, even more beautiful than you remembered it. And this is beauty all the way through, soul, being, her huge heart that has seen so much sorrow. What a Lady, and you need to thank God often for all of this wonder that's come into your life.

Sent 7 a.m., 7-15
Good Morning, John.
I am filled with the wonder of your love. I hope you are feeling the same about my love for you. May God bless the magic that happens when we are together. Joan

Afternoon of 7-15

To answer your question about June 29 to July 6 early a.m., my vote is to wait and see about the 3rd night. We might want it.

As for my world, a lot of that will depend on how visible you are willing to be. We can explore my Island, see my church, check out the Beach Club, take walks around my neighborhood or through some of our many parks. I will show you the Bellevue Arts Museum. We'll go to Kirkland which I love in the summer. You can walk along the lake there. There is a park right on the water, lots of restaurants, art galleries and interesting people watching goings on in that charming town. We can go out to dinner. We could even go to Snoqualmie Falls Lodge for lunch or dinner. My former reticence to that was because it is a romantic hotel. I was worried about the implication. I've changed my thinking. Of course, we can just stay here. We don't seem to have any problem finding things to do just being together.

I had a hard time sleeping again last night. Woke up after about four hours and spent the rest of the night reliving the evening. Lovely remembrances but I crashed after lunch and slept for nearly two hours. Then I washed a few windows, watered my many pots, and now I am going to change for the party at B.A.M. which is at six. I am going alone. Wish I could take you along *and* introduce you to all my friends and the world of art. You will, of course, be in my mind and heart throughout the evening. Leading exercise this morning was a real challenge. They would have been scandalized if they could have read my thoughts.

You are my love, Joan

8:30 p.m., 6-15
Hurriedly tonight, I agree with your ideas about our week together.

Last evening was the most memorable of *my life*, Joan, I will cherish the memories always.

Got to run, sorry. Good night. ILY

8:30 a.m., 6-16
Subj: Good Morning

Your words the other night, speaking of your past, you may not even remember them but I'll never forget as I looked into those soft brown eyes of yours: "There was no one to make love to me." I've thought about that for hours and it seems like an indictment of my stupidity as a college kid, not to "try harder" to win your love *then,* but I can only now try to make it up to you, Joan. Loving you as I do and *making love* to you are two different things, of course, and I know all about that. But you can never doubt that you have my love in whatever way I can express it to you.

How I do love you. John

6-15 10:46 p.m.
Good Morning

Hi John, Unless you are still awake at 10:30, or there abouts, you won't get this till morning. I just got home and, as always, checked the computer for your goodnight message. It was there as I expected.

The party at the museum was a huge success. Everyone raved about the show and in fact all the different galleries. I think you will like it too. This looked world class. I can hardly wait to read the papers. I am sure we are back on track. Museum parties always have wine and food. Tonight the food was very substantial. There are little tables set up so people can sit, but it is casual even when people are dressed up in "festive" clothes as they were tonight. Sometimes they use the stand up tall tables, but tonight you could sit if you found a spot. There was a band playing a little too loudly for comfortable conversation. I don't know why they don't tone the music down for occasions such as this. People mill around visiting and eventually go up to the second and third floors to view exhibits. One of the docents I know took me on a sort of private tour to practice the information she will be giving on her tours during the Teapot Exhibition. I saw lots of people I know, so it was comfortable and fun for me in spite of being alone. It is sort of like being with old high school friends.

Time for bed. My afternoon nap helped me get through the day. I still have some catching up to do. We'll see if I get through this night without spending half of it awake thinking of you. I doubt it, but at least the thoughts will be about something wonderful.

ILY2, Joan

John's note: As I re-read this wonderful Joan-prose, I'm reminded of how many times I joked with her, in our married life, that she should have been with me in the CIA! Joan had a remarkable visual memory, as her many accounts suggest. She could walk into a home, say, for an afternoon of bridge, a home she had never visited before, and come home to me and describe every visible detail: the entrance foyer, the house plants on display tables, the carpeting, the types of chandelier and other lighting, the stairways, how the windows faced, the napkins on the hostess' table, the sterling silver pattern. She always said that her best sense was "visual" and indeed it was, but I doubt that she realized how far above other "observers" her skills had taken her. I told her that if she had been with me in the CIA, bugging and cameras would not have been necessary: Just send Joan into a room—and no one would deny her stunningly beautiful entry—and she would return later and write a detailed report, totally without error!!

Hi, again,

Sorry for all the confusion, although hearing your voice made it worth it for me. You sounded remarkably alert for one just waking up.

It was your message last night that I zapped this morning, I had the other two. Thank you for sharing your evening, I so wish I could have been there. It's going to be difficult to choose what to do with that "extra" day now that I've carefully read your "list" of things to do in Your World. Wow, I'm impressed, but then I've been impressed beyond words for the past 90 days or so. (Is that all the longer it's been, remarkable?!!).

I didn't mean to say that you were "indicting" me, when I used that word. It's just that I beat myself up over those days so long ago, so many bad choices and the Word says *I* have to account for them, but only His grace makes that possible. And *your* grace where I'm concerned. How much that means to me, Joan, I can't describe it.

I want you to know, again, how you're in my prayers and thoughts virtually every waking moment. The intensity is unbelievable and I love every moment of it! Hard to concentrate on my job, but I can manage that. I love you so much, Joan, and am *so* proud of you and all that you do for others. I hope someone took your picture last night!! I must go for now.

Eternal Love, John
John

5:30 p.m., 6-16
It was wonderful having you wake me up. I couldn't imagine how late it was. I had slept only about four hours after I got to bed last night and was still awake after six this morning reliving Tuesday evening. I must have fallen asleep and had another several hours. Hooray, especially when you turned out to be my alarm clock. I love hearing your voice, ANYTIME.

The three last messages have been forwarded. It was the one I sent last night at ten thirty, The "Good Morning" one that told you next Wednesday is fine. That must be the one you zapped.

Today I have an at home day. I need it. Tomorrow there is another party at the Museum. This one is a tea from two to four for the Guilds and Docents. Of course I'll do the exercise class in the morning, and the evening is the "Couples Bridge and Annual Salmon Bake" at the Beach Club. The salmon is cooked in a pit on the beach, I think it is sort of a slow smoke process, but it is always excellent. A couple of men members do the cooking which takes hours. Women bring either salads or desserts. Escalloped potatoes, simple hors d'oeuvres and wine are provided.

This bridge group started out being husbands and wives. I think I may have told you that as many people aged and lost spouses, either through death or divorce, they could play with someone who was not a spouse. Either sex. I have played with a variety of people.

The MI Beach Club has a beautiful setting. It faces Mt. Rainer and the Renton area from the very Southeast part of the Island. I am close to the very Southwest part. I think I told you that at age 60 one is able to give back his membership to this club, keep all privileges except voting and mooring a boat, and pay half-price dues for the rest of your life. That is what I do. It is sort of funny though. I still pay the same amount that we paid when Cliff was still alive, so I guess I am still paying for two. I guess I do that for the Washington Athletic Club, too, but that I hold on to because dues should be free next year, after 50 years. The Beach Club has six outside tennis courts. I used to play every day in the summer. There is a pickle ball court, a big swimming pool with sort of grandstand seating, big play area for swimming, boat moorage, and a long area for lake swimming, sun bathing and picnicking. The clubhouse has a kitchen, but no regular food service. Meals have to be catered or cooked by members. I guess I am telling you all this to fill you in on my world. I will show you.

I started writing this a while ago. In between, I discovered that you had sent me another message, so I know that you got what I forwarded and all is well. It is about time for my cleaning gal to arrive. I'll send this off. I loved your "Good Morning" message. But then I love so much about you . . . . warts and all. Joan

6:30 p.m., 6-16
Sweetheart, I just picked up your latest message. I've been thinking about you all day, and imagining our future. The way I hope it could be.

I am so in love with you. It fills my whole being. My eyes filled with tears of happiness Tuesday night. I felt like yours did too. WE didn't talk about it, but I felt it.

My picture did get taken at the party last night, along with two of my friends. It is possible that it might get into the Seattle Weekly, I think that is it. I never see that publication, but the guy who took the picture took our names and our history with the museum, and said he would try hard to get it published.

I want us to be together. It feels so right.

My love and my prayers are always with you,

Joan

6-17, 8:00 a.m.
My Most Precious,

A couple of things to add to that checklist I left with you Tuesday: The candles you had on the table, please bring them. That was such a special meal and there's a lot of meaning in those candles for me—please. I'll have a cool box with ice in it and then we'll move everything into the MH fridge before we head out from the Puyallup fairgrounds.

I plan to ask my local butcher about fresh crab this time of year, you might do the same next time you're grocery shopping, just to get an idea if it's likely to be available in Ocean Shores. I'm going to see if they have a Web page, maybe that will give us a hint. If not crab, I'm sure your wonderful mind will come up with something special.

Thank you *so much* for the beautiful descriptions of your gala evening and "your world" at the Beach Club. It's a world I've never seen but there's still hope for this old geezer if he'll just stay well. And with the motivation he has nowadays, that is virtually guaranteed!

I will also see if the Seattle Weekly has some possibilities on line. One never knows although those pubs usually want a credit card to give you very much electronically.

Tears of joy and rapture on Tuesday, absolutely. No need to speak of anything in those moments of pure bliss, all the "talking" is sensual and lovely and the way God designed us. It just blows me away to think that this is finally happening to me and that you are just as thrilled about it as I am. It's a wager I wouldn't have made at any odds just a few months ago.

John

11:30 a.m., 6-17

I think we're going to have to force ourselves to mostly *talk* on Wednesday because I really want to hear from your lips to my ears about the possibilities for those days after we come back from the beach. So much to choose from and so little time. It will require great restraint because the hugs are so compelling, but let's give it a try, hmmmm?

I am so wound up about you, Joan, I can hardly stand it. How can this be possible in someone my (your) age?? What have we done to (for?) each other? So beautiful, so precious, so unique. How I do love you so.

Sorry, must close again. John

4:30 p.m., 6-17
My Darling,

This has been a most hectic day, and I am due to leave for the Beach Club in half an hour. I just got home from the museum lady party, sort of a tea party. First thing on my agenda was rushing to the computer and you. Thank you for three beautiful messages. I'll read them over again when I come home tonight. It will probably be after midnight, so this will have to hold you until tomorrow. I am sorry.

I did my exercise class. Had to go shopping for dessert ingredients and go to the recycle. Then I rushed home to make a pie to take tonight. Changed into my tea party clothes, went to pick up a friend but was nearly trapped in my driveway by the landscaper's truck. They had mowed my lawn and gone on to one of the neighbors. They always park along the road above my driveway. Today they were in my space to get out, so that slowed me down. I was late and getting frantic, but I got out. Now I'm short on time again. Some days are like that. It doesn't mean I haven't been thinking about you. That is a constant. I went over the BAM Tea Pot exhibit again today and imagined being there with you. Lots of them are really funny, some are rather porno, but acceptable as art.

All are entertaining and it is wonderful to see the imagination of the various artists. You will see.

Your words of love keep me going. Thank you for loving me. I am filled with joy because of it. I love you so, John.

8:50 p.m., 6-17
Good evening!
I don't know where you get all this energy, I admire you so. But you are such a joy to be around, I know your friends look forward to your company. Do sleep well, even if late. I love you so. John

Sent 9:30 a.m., 6-18
A break in my office routine, out comes my laptop. Now I can say good morning, knowing (hoping) that you are still sound asleep at 9:30. Last night I had these visions of you collapsing at 1 a.m., thoroughly drained but happy about such a successful culmination of all your hard work. What a Lady!! I also get nervous when you talk about getting home so late, understanding that you are alone. *Please* do be careful.

About the time you were collapsing into bed, I was waking up for the day, about 0230, unable to get back to sleep with all the beautiful visions that are by now so easy to conjure. I finally drifted off about 5 for a half hour, then up and at 'em. My group is having a tough time with a writing piece, the subject never seems to change, but I'll cope. And Washington's computer has been down for two days, making it impossible for us to communicate with hqs. Not good.

Rest as you can this weekend, Sweetheart. We'll be praying for each other in church on Sunday, as usual. Madly in love, how else to say it? John

9:30 a.m. (or so), 6-18
Good morning. I got out of bed at about 9:30, and headed for the computer, even before I brushed my teeth. I reread yesterday's messages from you and discovered a word I didn't remember seeing before. "Rapture." It's perfect, I looked it up to be sure. "Rapture," it says it all.

I am so glad you have mailed me the article from the Seattle Times. I haven't seen it. The BAM Board President told me yesterday at the tea party that there were great stories about the museum in both the P.I. and Times. I meant to pick them up on my way home, but I was in such a rush, I didn't have time. The Times probably will be here by 2:30 this afternoon.

The Salmon Bake was good. Marcia and I won third place at bridge and split our $5.00 winnings. It was well after midnight when we got back to my house and a little while before she left. It was 2:00 not 1:00 when I got into bed, but I did sleep soundly through the night.

Tomorrow I will sing in church, thinking of and praying for you. After church, I'll be going to an all afternoon party/barbeque at my niece's house. Her youngest daughter will be graduating from high school next week. This is a party to honor her and celebrate the graduation. There will be family members and assorted young and old friends. It will be a good occasion.

This afternoon I have to go out in the yard and cut/saw up a bunch of branches Libby pulled out of a huge hazelnut bush. They have been lying there for weeks. I have to clean up before the "Late Bloomers" arrive on Tuesday. It is going to be so nice to have a vacation soon, a relaxed time when we can do what we want, when we want, and just be together.

Thank you for your beautiful words of love. You warm me through and through. You are my love.

Joan

9 p.m., 6-18 (Sat)
Subj: Good Night Kiss
It is coming your way through my thoughts and my love. I am so glad you called. The sound of your voice gives me chills and thrills. This relationship is so different from anything I have ever had. I think the difference is an absolute God-given love. There is a power to it that I have never felt before. I feel that we have been especially blessed.

God bless you, keep you safe in his care, heal you completely, make you strong again, and let you love me as I love you.

Joan

Sun a.m., 6-19
Before I head for church.

I think our relationship reached another level yesterday when you explained *why* you chose that gorgeous outfit you wore Tuesday evening. That's the kind of trust and intimacy that means *so* much to me, Joan, and I'm so grateful that it comes so easily to you. I love you so, my Sunshine. I know you'll have a great day.
John

About 8 p.m., 6-19
Joan,

Your "Good Night Kiss" message brought a welling of emotions, you are *so* precious to me. I hope you don't tire of hearing that, but the words are precise. Look it up in Matthew (13: 45-46), the story of the pearl of great price: precious = priceless. The man gave everything he had to acquire it. That's where I am with you. We must talk about this on our "vacation."

Good night, my Most Precious. Wednesday isn't far off. John

CHAPTER 9

Joan's Dilemma

7:30 p.m., Sun 6-19
Hey, John

Help! This absolutely honest, honorable woman has just turned into a liar! Nothing like a family party to catch you off guard. I was happily enjoying the event when my niece asked, "You are coming to my birthday party, aren't you?" Her birthday is July 1. I replied that I couldn't because I was going away. Then a barrage of questions from her, my sister *and* Libby. Where, when, with whom? I said I was going to Ocean Shores with old high school friends. They know I go to the 1st Thursday lunch thing, so that seemed logical, and only my sister knows who any of that group is, except for Libby who is aware that your name is a household word. But my niece was persistent. She says I promised to come for her birthday, because we were going to celebrate with chocolate and the special red wine she bought when we went to Sonoma. I can't remember promising that. Your offer was much better.

Anyway, I think I stayed cool and stuck to my guns, but Libby kept staring at me with a knowing look. She, I am sure, has been aware of how many e-mails we exchange. She might even have read some of them. I don't know. I may get more questions, but nothing is going to change my mind or my plans. I am actually a little amused by all this. Maybe I enjoy the excitement. I'm not sure. I want to say I LOVE THIS MAN AND I WOULD RATHER BE

WITH HIM THAN ANYWHERE ELSE! I hope this isn't too upsetting to you. Any ideas?

Other than that, the day was fine. I drove my convertible, top down. It was a "Mexican Fiesta" theme with a Pinata that the little kids had fun with and lots of good Mexican food which my niece had cooked. Colorful decorations, too. My graduating great niece got lots of presents which she opened. The weather was perfect. No booze was served.

I hope your day was a little less eventful than mine. It does stir me up to have to cope with unexpected happenings. You are an expert. I am not, but nothing is going to keep me from our reserved time together.

I love you, John. You can count on that.

Joan

9 a.m., 6-20
Sweetheart:
I'm *sort of* laughing at this myself, except the part about Libby's awareness which I don't mind so long as she's cool with mom's having a "friend." You *could* go to your niece's party, of course, if it's in the afternoon or evening as I can get you home by noon or so if you're willing to get up *really* early. (Hmmmm?) But, if we want that third night possibility, then you're stuck with me. In either case, you're going to be questioned sooner or later about "Ocean Shores."

And is your family likely to expect you to be involved with them at some point during the period July 2-5? We haven't addressed that specifically but you should think it over. We'll go over this carefully Wednesday.

I've got to run, again, Sweetheart, wish I could write more. Maybe another note or two today, after the team finishes its day's work.

John

Sent about 3:30 p.m., 6-20
Subj: Cover Story
"We never stop working for you," goes the ad. That's how my mind is running today and this may sound outlandish at first read but please think about it, as I will.

If we ever need to explain to others our "connections," (phone calls, especially, e-mails, my visits to your home) we're following our "professional interests" and are working on a *strictly-business* deal to publish a series of (books, pamphlets, whatever) where you're the illustrator and I'm the writer. That's the bare-bones idea, and we can enlarge on it if/as/when needed. We can discuss this later, let your imagination run with it. It was your idea, remember, that we someday publish our love letters, after cleaning them up, as I think you put it.

The logic of this, it seems to me, is that no one in our high school class, especially, would ever think that I could "win you over." (What could she see in *him*?) Especially if you were to just laugh it off and insist it's strictly a business deal: We appreciate each other's intellect and talent, but that's absolutely *all*. The guys claim I "light up" when you appear at our luncheons, and no doubt that's true, but no one has ever suggested it's reciprocal!

Maybe more later, but not certain. Sleep well, if I can't tuck you in later. ILY John

1:45 p.m., 6-20
Hi John, I just got home from the Monday busyness at church. Had to do a little shopping for my luncheon tomorrow. Now I have to cook for it.

First things first. I always have to check for your message. Your response to my slight panic last night note calmed me a bit. And, no, I don't want to get up early and rush back for my niece's birthday. I'll stick with the third night possibility and stay stuck with you.

The "Too Funny" fwd made me laugh all the way through it. Thanks. Now I am all primed to go to the kitchen and prepare for tomorrow.

Love you,

Joan

"Sweet dreams to you dear if dreams there be. Sweet dreams that carry you close to me. I wish I may, and I wish I might, so goodnight my lover goodnight." Those are words to one of the love songs from "The Music Man." I have been singing it to myself and thinking of you ever since I went to the recent performance of that musical. It is even in my mind in the early morning.

You entertain me John. I was fascinated by your afternoon message. You make me laugh out loud, not at you but with you. When you mentioned my idea for our possible collaboration on a book of our love letters, I have to take issue with your comment that I suggested cleaning up those letters for publication. I think the word I used was "polish." They may be getting a little bit more steamy, but it seems to me they are really pretty clean. I believe our relationship is all about love. The rest is frosting on the cake.

Come on, John. I can't believe your friends don't think I would find you worthy of my love. You have always been a leader all the way through school, and certainly in your fraternity and at U-Dub as well. Beyond that I am sure you have proven yourself. Those guys don't know the joy of being kissed and held by you, this amazing man. Would you like me to give a speech to convince them of the things I find wonderful about you? How about at the '47 class Mini-Reunion ???

Sleep well, My Darling. I can hardly wait till Wednesday. I know we must talk seriously about our plans and *stay upstairs* and drink coffee, but just being together is a joy. It will be good.

John's editorial comment here: Joan's lovely Mercer Island home was/is a bi-level rambler, with all the bedrooms on the lower level. "Upstairs" is the street/entry level, her family room, dining room, living room and kitchen.

I'll be up early, working on my lunch party, but I'll be waiting to hear from you.

I am filled with love for you,

Joan

5:15 p.m., 6-21
Dear Editor,

Thank you for helping me to clean up my act which clearly was not polished well enough. I've thought for some time that you're smarter than I am, certainly much *wiser.*

Silly, eh? Love-silly. I'm not ashamed of this 75-year-old body/ brain combination which has slipped its moorings lately over a brown-eyed beauty named Jo-an. Problem is, I can't boast of it to anyone but her, which will have to do for awhile, but not forever. There's a mystery of excitement in our future, I know. We need to explore it fully and we will do that soon.

Be there for me tomorrow and save my sanity. I know you will!

Zany,

John

7 p.m., 6-21
Hey, is it okay if I dress you in that same "Tuesday outfit" when I daydream about having you in my arms? Maybe you can bring it to the beach and wear it inside the MH only. Or do you have other outfits just as fetching?? Aren't I nosey? Laugh all you want, I'm sort of serious—until you tell me to get lost.

8 p.m, 6-21
John, I was way ahead of you . . . . or maybe not. I have been *thinking* about putting your favorite outfit in my suitcase. I will for sure now that you have made a special request. That may be the sexiest outfit I own which is why I wore it for you. I liked the result last time and hope it will be equally good the next. You can dream about that all you want. I do.

Tonight I am really tuckered. I have been waking on your schedule and going to bed on mine. I've got to try for early tonight, so I am in shape for your visit tomorrow. I am so glad I have that to look forward to, even though it will be far too brief. Next week will be only 7 days away. I can hardly wait. Then we can concentrate on US.

I will joyfully greet you tomorrow at about one o'clock, arms wide open and love in my heart.

I love you, John,

Joan

John spends several hours with Joan in her home, afternoon of 6-22

Evening, 6-22
Hi,
I kept running those words back over and over "if we don't like each other," and although we were sort of jesting I suppose that's what this upcoming week is really all about. Here I am thinking mostly about the "M" word, yet I have to admit that we probably need to look for more warts, too. It's hard to square that idea with the intensity of my love for you, Joan—I can't imagine learning *anything* about you that would change these deepest of feelings for you. But be warned that I plan to tell you about what others have told me over the years are my major shortcomings (well, one, anyway, I snore loudly) and we'll have fun dissecting each other. I hope my sense of humor is up to this.

Are you okay with the food list? I'll be adding a few things from my own fridge, you'll see what a yukky eater I can be.

Too short a time, today, and I know you felt the same. Try to get a little more rest in the days ahead, my Precious One.

Love you, love you, love you. John

Sent 8 p.m., 6-22
John, it is about 7:30 and I am still floating. It is always hard for me to come down to earth after you have been here with me. I can't imagine that we won't still like each other after our beach togetherness. No doubt, there could be sometime in the future that we would have a fight, but I sure can't see it now. WE are so on the same page and having fun being there.

I am intrigued to know what it is you like to eat. I probably should have asked before I planned what I would bring. I may have to educate you . . . or you me. Some women I know tell me their husbands are "Meat and Potato" guys. Boring! My Dad was that way. I escaped and did my own thing. However, I do my best to make the man I love as happy as possible, so whatever your weird food preferences may be I will consider them.

Snoring is acceptable. It is possible I do that too. One of the roommates I had on last year's Choir Tour said I snored a little. Cliff snored so loudly for years that he woke up his children down the hall. It stopped after he had his heart surgery. Speaking of Choir Tours, I was thinking today that maybe you and I can go together on the next one. The Director said maybe in three years from last.

My tomorrow schedule is this. At nine AM I will drive a group of my BAM Guild to Tulallip Shores to the summer beach home of a member for our June meeting. We go there every June. We all take salads for lunch and have a great time. I will get home around three. At four my sister will pick me up to go to the opening of the new show at the Museum of Glass in Tacoma. That is a great museum. I joined it before it opened. Now I have to go make my salad for the meeting and eat my dinner. I won't get to bed early tonight. Can you put up with this wart?

You made my day today, John, and I can't wait for the next together time. I am so excited. Love you. Joan

PS I'm not sure this is a wonderful goodnight message, but I hope you get it before you go to sleep. There is always so much to say when we are together and never enough time. I know you are more controlled than I about doing things according to schedule, and under the circumstances that is important. I get carried away and can't bear to let you go.

"Kitchen Talk" 11 a.m., 6-23
Quite seriously, if you fix it I'll eat it so long as it's not *too* spicy-hot. And if your soup yesterday was "hot" then I'm not worried.

I'm curious and excited to explore your cooking tastes and skills, Dear Lady. Don't expect too much latitude in a motor home, and expect "durable" (beat up) cups, plates, "silver," etc. I'll try to find you a coffee mug with minimum stains and if that's impossible we'll buy you a brand new one in Ocean Shores—or you could bring your own, to be real safe! I think I already warned that the wine "glasses" are clear plastic, which is handy when they fall off the shelf and onto the floor as happens sometimes in rough driving conditions.

You looked a little sad as I pulled out of the driveway yesterday and that saddened me, too. I think you're more tired than you realize and, face it, parting isn't fun for either of us.

More later today, I think.

I'll copy your house-entry instructions and figure out a place to conceal them well. That kind of evidence mustn't be handled idly! I'm flattered by your confidence to share that, I guess I've become kind of "family" without realizing it. And family love each other, don't they? My, oh my.

ILY,

John

3:30 p.m., 6-23
Hi, again,
I never responded to your Robert Preston lines (it was he, wasn't it, "The Music Man"?), loved that show but can't remember if I saw it on stage or somewhere on film. That and My Fair Lady rank at the top with me. One of these days we'll go together to an event like that. I've just never felt like going to those things by myself, and I can see that you take it in like breathing. I can't be envious, just proud and happy that you've been able to do those things, you're so deserving of them. Maybe a bit of that can rub off on me next week. Try to "rub," will you??

Is Tulalip Shores the same as LaConner? I think I may have mixed up those two in your recountings. I know LaConner and love the place, with its water and boats and open-air decks at the restaurants and all the friendly gawking that goes on there. I've been a few times when visiting the flower fields, where the *yellow* tulips are my favorites!

I'm tired just sitting here writing most of the day, after a half-hour walk this morning, and I imagine you scooting all over the place from nine til nine like you were a teenager all over again, making sure your lady-guests get the best views and best seats and just being a super hostess. After our week together I'll need that quiet week in Montana, with a bunch of *old* guys, just to recover.

Not sure I'll get another chance today, my Sunshine. Thinking of you constantly, which does get in the way of my "duties." But I'm lovin' it, as I do love you, so much.

John

3 p.m., 6-23
Sweetheart, I am the one squeezed for time this afternoon. I just got home from Tulalip Shores. It is on the water across from Camino Island, and we met and had our meeting and lunch at the waterfront summer home of one of our members. It was a perfect day. I drove three other people there and back. Now I'm tired, but Barbara and I are going to Tacoma to the opening of the new show at the Glass Museum. The party starts there at five. She will drive but I will meet her at my church parking lot for convenience. I'm not sure what time we'll get back. We may have dinner somewhere before we come home, so this may be the one and only message you get today.

I loved being with you yesterday if even for such a seemingly short time. Still have nice memories from that time. If this turns out to be it for today, sleep well, sweet dreams. I'll be thinking of you and loving you.

Joan

9:30 p.m., 6-23

Precious,

I've been thinking about your "schedule." I think it would tire a 40-year-old woman! I am so taken with you, Joan, imagining all the things you are doing. It's got to be tough on you, but I know you love it and so do I. John

9 p.m., 6-23
John, I was sitting here reading your two messages from today when another one just appeared. Perhaps you won't get this before you go to sleep, but just in case.

I loved the show at the Glass Museum. Both artists were there, both whose work I know and who used to bring things to sell at the auctions I chaired. One is a woman who was horribly injured in an automobile accident after I first knew her work.

179

She is crippled and had to learn to talk again. She was moving around via a machine she stood on, and she spoke about her work which is colorful and uplifting and displays her courage and determination to live fully in spite of her limitations. Very creative. She was inspiring. Her name is Ginny Ruffner

The other is a guy, about 48 now, who I watched blow glass at the Pilchuck School years ago. He was so handsome that every woman who saw him there that day swooned, and swooned again every time he walked into the museum. He is enormously successful now, and still good looking, but more mature. His name is William Morris and all my friends call him Billy. Not to his face, but I think many people did.

We didn't go out to dinner. There was plenty of food available at the party. We had to buy wine and had one glass each. For dessert they had huge cakes done up like pieces of art that simulated the artists' work. They sliced it up and passed it out. There was a musical combo that played good background music. The weather was so nice and we could see the mountain, so we did enjoy our evening.

I, however, am really exhausted. Much too much activity for one day.

So goodnight, My Darling. Thank you for your messages to me. I love you.

Joan

2:30 p.m., 6-24
Hi,
I figured you'd be exhausted when I saw how late you were going to the Glass Museum in Tacoma, traffic and all. The seniors' group from my church has been to the history museum for a couple of shows and then across and up the street for lunch. I think the last one was about Nine-Eleven, you may have seen that there or elsewhere.

I'm furious today with the Lib 5 on our Supreme Court and their Eminent Domain decision. Talk radio this morning was about impeaching them, or at least Ruthie.

Hey, Precious, please slow down, okay? And did you get any questions about Ocean Shores??

Your house entry instructions are under the seat cover in my beat up car, not likely to be searched any time soon.

Must go for now, you should have had at least one nap today before reading this. I love you, Joan, it's a constant state and never out of my mind.

John

5:30 p.m., 6-24
Hi, finally. I've had another busy day and just got home. Did the exercise class, then a few necessary chores at home, talked to the gal responsible for getting the art to the patron's party and arranging it and set up a time to meet with her at the museum this afternoon.

Libby took the day off. I had invited her to have lunch and see the exhibition at the museum. We did both the meeting and the tour together. She sat in at the meeting and actually came up with some good ideas. The children of all of us old women, who have worked for years on the Bellevue Arts and Crafts Fair and for the Bellevue Arts Museum, have been put to work in various ways since they were young. She thought it was normal.

I had no Ocean Shores questions from my sis last night or today. I sure was expecting there might be some. Heave a sigh of relief for today, at least.

My clock radio woke me this morning with that Supreme Court decision on Eminent Domain. I was mad. What is happening to our rights? It seems they are being slowly undermined. We need to fight back.

The Museum of History in Tacoma is a wonderful place. I really like it, but missed the Nine-Eleven exhibit. It seems that was somewhere in Seattle too, but I didn't go. Maybe it was because that day was so painful for me that I wasn't ready to relive it.

It was late when I finally got home. Libby wanted to do some shopping, so I agreed we would. That made the afternoon longer than expected, but good togetherness with her.

I am very worn out. On the drive home I kept thinking that all I wanted was to be in your arms. For me that is the most comforting, relaxing place I can be. I am still longing for that, but I guess I'll have to wait a while. Tomorrow and Sunday should be relatively quiet and at home except for church. Maybe I can catch up on relaxation.

I'm sorry I've let myself get overloaded with activities that have cut down on my computer time with you. I'll be better now. I hope you haven't felt deserted. You are in my heart and my thoughts through all my waking hours, and even when I am sleeping you are there. I love you.

Joan

8:30 p.m., 6-24
My Darling, I don't know what your evening plans are for tonight, but I want to be sure that you have a goodnight kiss from me. I will try to collapse early. I have been over the top for several days in a row.

Whatever is going on in our lives, I pray it will be good for both of us together. It has occurred to me that perhaps everyone assumed by my answers to questions about my niece's birthday that I would be at Ocean Shores only one day. I never gave a time. If they thought that, it is a blessing unplanned. I hope it is so.

My only concern is about my mail pick-up. I was going to ask my closest neighbor to pick up because it is a short time. I do it for her frequently, but she seldom for me because Libby does it. This time I thought she would be perfect cover, but I noticed this morning that they were packed and ready to leave. They go to Whistler frequently and school is just out, so I will try another neighbor. Other than that I am feeling pretty safe. I will spend the weekend preparing for our time together. I have made a list of what I am to bring. I will be completely organized by early Wednesday morning and eagerly looking forward to your arrival. Sleepy eyed, maybe, but sooooo happy that this is happening to me. This will be a never before kind of experience. It is major in my life to me, but something I feel is really important for us. And any way, I really do want to see how you handle those kites. I'll be surprised if I can do it, but I will try. If it pours rain and is windless, I can think of other things to do! I want this, John. I can hardly wait. If I did not love you so, this would never be happening. I hope you truly understand and believe that.

Goodnight, my dearest love,

Joan

8:45 a.m., 6-25
Hi, and good morning,
It's Saturday but I'm in my office most of the day, darn, lots of catching up to do before my friend arrives from D.C. to inspect this place. But his presence will mean my absence!

Yes, I DO understand and believe that, with all my heart.

"Rain?" Cooped up with me in the rain, for days? Hmmmm? I think we'd better both pray for sun and do our "cooping up" after it gets dark. We need balance and some serious thought, no kidding. Two futures at stake here, I'm thinking. Passion for sure, but clarity and realism, too. It will be the most important week of my life!
ILY, John

6:20 p.m., 6-25
"Rain?"
Hi John, have you been reading weather reports or do you just assume that at our Washington ocean sites it is likely to be that way? It is so beautiful at this moment that I have to hope we will catch at least some of the same next week.

I keep thinking about how hard it is to do anything but love you when I am with you, but that is partly because we have had such little time together. This will be different, and I will try hard to follow a sensible program of reality. I know we have much to discuss and figure out. That is of major importance to me too. I understand that and agree that we will stick to the plan you have set out. Pretty much.

I have spent this day quietly preparing for our tryst. It makes me feel like Romeo and Juliet only 60 years beyond them. I hope the finale is a lot different than theirs.

I felt that when the Oriole landed on my deck railing right after I had told you about it, it was a good omen. That was special. I wish you could have seen it.

I am so glad you called this morning. It truly made my day. I have felt warmly loved all day long. You do that for me. It is a remarkable all enveloping feeling. I am so happy, so excited to be looking forward to our special time together. A few months ago this would not have occurred to me, but suddenly life changed into a miracle. I believe it was meant to be. We will be sensible, realistic and thoughtful about our lives when we talk. I promise I will be. I think about it a lot and still feel we are on the same page. I *am* a realist, John, but I can dream dreams too. My love for you goes so deep.

Joan

9 p.m., 6-25

But even if it's sunny, we can hug on the beach! Thank you for understanding, as I knew you would. ILY John

8:30 p.m., 6-25
Goodnight My Darling, Sweet dreams. We'll be OK. I love you. Message again tomorrow. Hugs and Kisses,

Joan

Sometime 6-26
Hi, It was a Bullock's Oriole, beautiful to match the beauty of the one who saw it!

11:30 p.m., 6-26

Hi John, It has been a long day in which I haven't had the opportunity to get to the computer. Libby has been here since I got home from church. I had to go out to water all my dried up pots, cut back a few overgrown things and wonder if I'll ever catch up with my yard work again.

Summer usually is a time I have more time at home. This year seems different, probably because of commitments at the museum. I'm already organizing another meeting there for July 6th, at one o'clock for my guild and the "preparator," that's what they call the person who sets up for shows. You'll be on your way early, so I figured it was a good time. Now I have to call all the people.

Libby did ask a question or two about Ocean Shores today which actually made me relax a little more. She thought I was going to be there over the 4th. I told her I was leaving Wednesday and home on Saturday. She accepted that with no more questions, so I won't be concerned about her discovering that I'm gone and worrying about me. Oh, these tangled webs.

The weather report in the paper today shows Wed. and Thurs. as sunny. Of course, one never knows about the coast. But if it rains, we can read if we run out of talk, or even if we don't

185

just to be sure we keep that balance. I've even thought of bringing my paints, but that might be dangerous inside your motor home in case I might make an unpredictable mess that wouldn't clean up.

I'm lonesome. It seems the more I see you, the more I miss you when you are not here. Now I'm wondering about your trip to Montana. How long does it take you to get there? Where do you go? How long are you gone? Am I asking too many questions?

On my way into church today I spoke to a woman who I don't know well, but I do know she is a devoted birder. I told her about the oriole and she said they aren't on the Island very often, but once in a while a group will pass through. I feel blessed to have two in my yard.

Now I have to go call guild members about that meeting and fix my dinner. I know that I can't definitely expect to hear from you today, so don't worry if you can't connect. I won't like it, but I will survive. Love you, love you, love you, Joan

10:30 a.m., 6-27
Good morning, my Precious One,

It's 10:30 and I'm about to go to Dr. Ward for the scope exam, to see how all the chemo, etc., has done its job. I expect flying colors.

"Consumed" is a very good word, for both of us. I've never felt this way either, never, ever. I hope we can behave reasonably well over the next days and not behave as a couple of dopey would-be teenagers.

Looking ahead to day's end, I'm still really pressed to get everything ready for the Big Inspection, not sure I'll have time to write much.

I love you Joan, with every fiber. Gotta go to my doc.

John

2 p.m., 6-27
Hi, again.

Doc is "pleased," but to be safe wants me to get into a kind of "routine" with the same chemo treatments, once a week for three weeks, every two months or so. I wasn't expecting that, thought I'd have at least six months before the next exam, but I trust this man completely and would never question his judgment.

Let's face it, My Beloved, we're both a bit of damaged goods and maybe we're at least subconsciously enough aware of that that it propels us to this vice-grip passion we have for each other, time is so important. Just think of what's happened since April 6, when I hugged (but did not kiss) you. Less than 90 days!

Love flows on these electrons, I know you can feel it.

John

5:25 p.m., 6-27
Hey John, your descriptive powers are right on. Vice-grip passion is exactly what is happening. It makes me laugh to think of it that way, but it is so true. And I don't care. You are probably right about the reasons, too. We have to live each day and make the most of the time we have. No question. One of us is going to end up taking care of the other unless we both get into the same boat at the same time. I've been there, done that, and told myself never again. Then you came along and my whole perspective changed. I am a willing participant in whatever happens in our lives. This love is total joy to me.

This day, after all my obligations were fulfilled, I've been preparing for Wednesday. I've been collecting things you said to bring. I have stopped my paper, found a neighbor who will pick up my mail, checked lists and gathered things together, made the last of necessary phone calls about my next BAM meeting, shopped for food items that I need to prepare for our lunch and first night dinner, found a birthday card for my niece who expected me to share her birthday party, put the candlesticks and candles where I won't forget. I'll be ready!

I just read the "Song of Songs" in *The Message.* It was easier to understand in that version and I could really relate to it having the feelings that surge through me now. Have you ever read it? I'll bring you that book.

If you can't connect tonight, I'll be all right. We are almost there, sweetheart. Sunshine or rain doesn't matter, being together does. I can hardly wait even though it will be soon. I love you so.

Joan

Hi, Precious, just time to remind you, I expect to phone you around 0830-45. My love for you just has to give in to some sleep tonight, I'm sure it will.

John

CHAPTER 10

Finally, On the Beach

Here, is a four-day break in the e-mails. John and Joan are at last on the beach at Ocean Shores, in his motor home, taking long walks on the mostly-empty beaches and talking carefully and honestly about the "M" word. Joan would say later that she considered this to be her wedding night, so thoroughly wrapped were they in each other. Among several new things John learned about Joan, in their long and intimate conversations, was an explanation of her reference in her very first e-mail to him about "three times" learning of cancer: She had endured two radical mastectomies, in 1994 and 1997, and a successful melanoma excision some time later. Of course neither of them thought of it at this time of their utter happiness: How much longer would the cancer remission continue?

7-2, 9 p.m.
Sweetheart,

You'll no doubt be in bed as I write this (beginning at 9 p.m.), we're both so tired from loving each other so much these past few days, what an absolute joy it has been. I've never known such ecstasy, such happiness, such a feeling of fulfillment to be with you in these circumstances. For me (for you, impossible) it was as though God backed up the clock just a little, to give me a glimpse of what might have been had I not so fatally squandered those moments of opportunity so long ago. Perhaps this is His justice, requiring of me a humility of honor, kindness and respect toward you that I could never have for another human being. I think I sometimes make you uncomfortable with my words of honor and admiration and adoration, but I can't help it, I'm driven to say those things, sometimes as awkward as they may sound.

I know our union is now a sure thing. When my contract is up, we'll head for Honolulu, not that far off and most certainly worth the wait. We've had good talks about this and I know how each of us feels.

It was wonderful to hear your voice on the phone, even though we had spoken face to face a few hours earlier. And I'll be lucky to get much out of the sermon in the morning, thinking of being with you in only another hour or two.

God bless you, My Darling, and *please* sleep well.

I love you so much,

John

7-3, 5 a.m.
Good morning, already!

To bed at 10, up at 0430, what else is new?
I'll be phoning about 0945 to suggest you open your e-mail and you'll find this message and two others, from last night. See, I have this habit—

You can be thinking about this as I drive over later this morning.

I love you, John

Sent about 11 p.m., 7-3
Good evening, Precious One (probably morning when—if—you see this).
Now it's 10:30 p.m. and I'm finishing up my devotion for the Seniors' group luncheon next Friday. It will be held at a lakeside home and it truly is a beautiful setting. I was reminded of that

same kind of beauty this afternoon, in God's creation, of what we saw together and also in you, the beauty of your spirit and your being, Joan. That you lavish your love on me is *almost* beyond belief, but not quite. Yes, we do have fun together but I think it is more than that, kindred spirits, yes, and two people who need and have found each other late in life but not so late that we cannot start afresh and do our best, in God's will, to help each other and as many others as He will place in our pathways. I believe this is so and I know you do, too. I think we have a wonderful future before us and I promise to do all that I can to make the very most of that future with you by my side and I by yours.

I love you, Joan.

John

11:03 p.m., 7-3
My Darling,

Thank you for sending those beautiful words that I will have in my mind and my heart as I fall asleep tonight. I just had to check, and I am glad I did. They are too precious to miss. Your devotion was lovely and I prayed the prayer you wrote. I thank God for you, John, and for the love we share. How happy can one person be? I feel so blessed.

It is my usual late hour, but I'll be there to open the door for you in the morning. You must be asleep by now, and I hope that you will awake completely rested and ready for another wonderful day together. My love is deep and true.

Joan

Sent 11:15 p.m., 7-3
Important news, forgot to tell you earlier today:

First sighting this morning of two baby swallows in their box, with their little heads stretched out the opening, with both parents feeding them, I would say frantically. There likely are one or two others.

Thank you again. I love you.

John

At this point in their story, John spends the July 4 holiday with Joan at her Mercer Island home, after returning from Ocean Shores. By a long-standing commitment he drives to Western Montana to spend a few days with old fishing-buddy friends. On his return he visits Joan at her home on his way back to his.

7/12, 8:22 p.m.
John, It is a little after nine. I hope you are sound asleep and catching up on much needed rest. I wish I had just sat you down and wrapped my arms around you today. I do appreciate your help, your gentleness, your kindness and your willingness to make my life easier. I love it when you smile and when we laugh together. The love in my heart for you wells up and fills my being. I hope you can feel it. I will sleep well tonight because of it, and because you were here with me today. That is always a blessing. We will have lots of days ahead when we can laugh and love and be happy. I count on that and pray for it. God bless you. I love you. Joan

6:30 p.m., 7-13
My most Precious,

Thank you for your most encouraging and loving note, which I have only now been able to read (6 pm, Wed), with my laptop crash now fixed, about $150 worth of "fix." I slept for 7 hours last night, and have felt pretty good today but I need to fatten up a bit, down to 161, too light. I feel much too far away from you, Joan, but I do sense your love and your protective prayers. I do love you, Sweetheart.

John

6:45 p.m., 7-13

Did I thank you for the very tasty muffins and the delicious sandwich? You are a genius in that well-worn kitchen of yours. I look forward to helping and now and then doing a solo performance for *you only.*

ILY

7-13, 8:40 p.m. "Tonight"
Dearest, You can cook in my well worn kitchen, and it surely is that, any time you feel inspired to do so and I will love it. I can tell by our conversations that you know and appreciate food and can cook. Perfect. That kitchen will become not mine but ours in the not too distant future, I pray.

I am also concerned about my much too soft and worn out mattress and want to correct that problem. However, I really need your help when I go shopping for a new one. Do you think we could possibly make a date to shop together for that? Pretty bizarre? It needs to be right. Yes?

There are so many things I wish we could be sharing right now and in the days to come. It is hard to wait, but it is worth the effort. I smile to myself a lot lately, because I have such happy hopes for our future. I wonder if my friends might think something must be going on to change me. Probably people don't notice, but I feel a lot different than I did a few months ago. There is magic in my world now. You have made that happen.

I love You, Joan

9:30 p.m., 7-13 "A little more"
It is almost 10:30 now. Time to trundle off to my squishy mattress. I hope you are tucked in and sleeping soundly. You fill me with joy. Believe it. Joan.

10 p.m., 7-14
A mattress-buying tryst? Why not!? Somehow I'm giggling over this whole idea. Maybe you've decided you don't like soft and squishy any more than I do. Can you see these two *old people* flopping all over mattresses in a department store? That would be a real test of composure, wouldn't it?

6:30 p.m., 7-14
John, I am so glad your computer is well again. I thought it might take days. Sorry I haven't sent a message earlier. I got your nice long note earlier when I got home, shortly before my beautiful house cleaning gal arrived. That is not a good time to be writing.

This morning I had to go shopping for some stuff to consider for use in presenting the art at the Patron's Party. Then back to the museum to meet again with the "Preparator." She liked what we brought, so that is one problem solved. Then I hurried home by 12:30 to grab some lunch and let Jessica and her vacuum and mops in the door. While she was cleaning, I went down those railroad tie steps to the cul de sac and trimmed the ivy off the water meter. Those steps are overgrown with weeds and ivy, so I guess I'll go work on that after I finish this. I then came back in the house and drew all the curtains, let down the bamboo blinds and opened all the doors. It is getting hot. I am appreciating your help with those blinds.

It tickles me that you are amused at the vision of us testing mattresses. I know that old mattress of mine is beyond its last legs. I'm not sure I'll go for the *most firm*, but those are supposed to be best for bad backs. Your pillow looks like a bed of nails to me. You must enjoy pain. Anyway, if you want a say in this we probably had best wait a bit. It might look a little goofy if we went shopping now, especially if we ran into some of my friends, but it sounds like fun to me, and I *am* tired of being squishy. Yesterday I picked blueberries. There was another bird under the net when I approached the bushes. I thought I'd have to try to get him out, but he escaped through an opening in the top which I hadn't been aware of. It will probably be a couple of days before there will be enough ripe for picking again.

Time to go tackle the weeds and ivy on the steps. I'll be thinking of you as I work.

Loving you,

Joan

8:30 p.m., 7-14
Hi,

You can't imagine how I long to be with you, all the time, in every room in your home, following you around like a puppy (well for a few days, anyway, until you get tired of it!). Three months ago I could never have dreamed I'd be this way. It seems like a dream but I know it's very real and only a few months before we are together for as long as God gives us.

Have a very good night, please. ILY John

8 p.m., 7-14
John, I just told our love story to people who are long time best friends who live in Laguna Beach, California. They called me because it is my wedding anniversary and they never forget. Don was Cliff's best friend and best man at our wedding. I dated him before I dated Cliff. I told them we love each other and hope to be married in a few months. They were delighted. They immediately said to come visit them, and I know we could go tomorrow and stay together in their guest room and it would be fine. I went twice last year to visit them and had a wonderful time. They are probably the only people I can share with who are absolutely safe and supportive.

Anyway, my sweet, I have to let you know what I do. No secrets between us, ever.

John, I need and want to be with you, too. All the time. I keep thinking of how right it seemed to be together for those blessed seven days. For me, there was no sense of having to figure it out. Every thing seemed comfortable and as natural as if we had been together for years. The thought brings tears to my eyes. I can't believe that happens to many couples. This is so special. No doubt about it. You are my love.

Joan

Sent 2 p.m., 7-15
Wow! I am absolutely delighted that you were able to share our story, Sweetheart, for certain. And with special friends, that is *so* important. Thank you for using your best judgment. I trust you, completely: NO secrets!!

Good workout at Bally this morning, I needed it. But I look skinny and flabby in the mirror. You're my model there, I need to whip the old bod into shape to look as good, at 75, as yours. Impossible? Probably. Enough time? Only God knows.

Must go. Love you endlessly.

John

4:30 p.m., 7-15

It is disappointing that this day turned out to be rainy. After about an hour and a half pulling weeds and blackberry vines yesterday evening, I realized that those steps and the surrounding area are going to take days of work and I'm counting on this weekend to proceed. Maybe tomorrow. I should have a whole day free.

Another reason the rain is a drag is because the MI Beach Club TGIF party is best on the beach, now it will have to be in the clubhouse which isn't as much fun. Some friends are picking me up at ten to six. I wish I could take you along.

If I am complaining and sounding grumpy, it is because I am lonely for you. You add sunshine to my life when you are here. Lots of it. It was so great to be together and I got greedy wanting more. And more and more. I pray that will happen soon.

In the meantime, I think you should start getting a chocolate shake every day to add back a little weight, and/or a great big dish of vanilla ice cream with chocolate sauce, sliced banana, whipped cream and cherries. Many people would envy you the opportunity. If you were here I would work hard at filling you with extra calories . . . healthy ones.

I am glad you were glad that I told my friends about us. It was a relief to talk to someone and have them be so accepting. I keep dreaming of what lies ahead for us. They are wonderful, hopeful dreams. I know they will become a reality.

I think you can tell that I love you. Joan

7:30 p.m., 7-16
Hi,
Check your voice mail. I blew that one! Christmas is no doubt a special family time for you and yours and I shouldn't presume to change that. I detected a bit of reluctance in your voice at my impulsive suggestion so you can see how easy it is to win an "argument" with me.

Must go, again, darn.
John

6 p.m., 7-16
Sweetheart,

After we talked on the phone I lay down on the family room couch for a bit, then went out and picked today's supply of blueberries. After that I got my gardening tools and a container and headed for those steps again. I didn't come in until almost seven, put a pork chop on to cook and came down to connect with you. I worked hard on those weeds and ivy, got a heavy load to carry back up to dump in the yard waste container. Now I am tired, satisfied that I accomplished something worthwhile for the day and ready to relax for the rest of the evening. I only wish you were here so we could sit on the couch in the family room wrapped in each others arms. Dream of that. I will.

Sleep peacefully, my beloved, Joan

Hi. It is after 9:30 7-16 and I have eaten and been thinking about you. I hadn't listened to your phone message until now, but it made me giggle because you get so concerned about saying the wrong thing to me. HEY, I understand that we all have ideas that pop into our heads and later seem to be mistakes. I never thought twice that it wasn't a neat idea to go to The Desert for Christmas. I like the fact that you are thinking ahead for us. I am too. I am open to all kinds if suggestions. Besides, I am really a down to earth lady. It is fun to have you think I am your "goddess," but I am really your friend, your companion and your lover and I like the way we laugh together over the most amazing things. That is even better to me.

I seem to have written a lot today. I need the connection I think. Not being able to touch you is agonizing. Words help some. It is getting late and I have to throw a few dishes in the dishwasher and go to bed. Church in the morning. Goodnight my sweet Frog Prince with all the warts that disappeared when the Princess kissed him.

ILY, Joan

5:45 p.m., 7-17
Hi, Sweetheart,

Goddess is with a capital "G," Dear Lady, whenever it applies to You. That's my rule. But you really are a fun and down-to-earth woman (with a whole lot of class at the same time) and I love you the more for it. The Desert and your *birthday*, why not think about that?! You've mentioned that combination before.

I love you, Joan.

John

PS: Is that what happened to those warts?? I guess "Princess" is okay so long as you're the one using the term. I still prefer Goddess and you should get used to it, even though it's a Greek idea. :)

7-17, 7 p.m.

John, It was a good church service this morning, although summer church is never as full as when we are in our September-May routine. Fortunately, many of my best friends were there and we went to "Anna's" for breakfast as usual. Someday you will be joining us there. I know you will be accepted and have a good time talking to these interesting guys with their varied experiences and they will find you equally interesting. I know you are going to fit in easily with this church and with my friends. It will be almost instantaneous once we are together. You have so much to offer, John. It will be good, never fear.

John, I just picked up your latest message. The fairy tale says the princess kissed the frog and he suddenly turned into a prince. No goddess is mentioned but I sure like the idea you've given to the word, Greek or not! I love you John and look forward to our being together for whatever time God gives to us. The thought fills me with delight.

Joan

8:30 p.m., 7-17 "Evenings"
John, I've finished dinner, need to clean up my kitchen and head for bed, but re-reading your message, I find that you were asking if all evenings were available for getting together. The answer is yes, however it will be very hard for me to allow you to leave if you show up in the evening. Squishy mattress, bed of nails pillow

not withstanding, the temptation might be too much for me. How strong are you????

XOXO Joan

At this point in their story John is blindsided by a critical Inspector's Report, generated by his old friend who had come from Washington, D.C. to look at John's writers' group. (It was that visit that made it possible for John and Joan to "escape" to Ocean Shores, where they decided to marry.) The report was based largely on the inspector's conversations with a disgruntled group member for whom John earlier had submitted a marginal Performance Evaluation. John feels obliged to defend the rest of his group, all of whom are doing excellent work, and he also worries that, as this is his last-ever work for the Agency, his own legacy may be threatened. His concerns and his mood are reflected in his and Joan's on-going exchange of e-mails.

CHAPTER 11

Correcting the "Record"

Sent about 5 p.m., 7-18, after reading the inspector's report.

Joan,
I think my phone call probably put us both in an awful emotional state, and just when everything was looking so positive. I promise you I will weather this and set the record straight. I've been around Agency politics long enough to know how these things happen, and, usually, how to fix them. Trust me. I love you Joan, and it's your never-failing love that will see us through this.

A.M. 7-20, "Loving You"
MY beloved,

This is much more difficult for you than for me. I pray that you will be vindicated and the truth will be recognized by everyone. You are such an amazing person to me that I know you have much to offer no matter into what situation you are placed. You will fit into my world as you have been able to fit in *around* the world. I have no doubt about that, nor do I have any about the fact that I love you and need you and want you to be, not a part of my life, but my *whole* life.

I love you for so many reasons, John. These are just a few. I love you because you can casually change your pants in front of me without thinking twice, just because we are so comfortable with each other. I love you because you will forever feel inclined to laugh when someone mentions Eggs Benedict. You are pure fun, pure joy. I love your manners, the way you make me feel cared for and appreciated, I love your intelligence and knowledge of the world and the way you share it with me. I love the way we are on the same page about so many things, and the way you make me feel that I am smart and capable and doing good in the world. I feel blessed that you love me, John, and thrilled beyond belief that that you have chosen me. I only wish that our permanent togetherness could start right now.

You have had a difficult day. There will be more. Just hang on to my love and we will get through this together. And please let's figure out ways to be together in the interim. I need you so.

Goodnight my love, Joan

6:20 p.m., 7-21
Sweetheart,

Thanks for that wonderfully supporting note, my Precious. I can read it carefully now. I know we're "linked" through all of this, for however long it takes. ILY

7:20 p.m., 7-21
Hey, to change the subject, which needs doing!

I'm just noticing in my office bookshelf a whole collection (4 "volumes") of just about everything Beethoven ever wrote, on 33 rpm records. Do you have a player for 33's? I don't but if you do I'll keep the collection and maybe we could occasionally listen together, something I haven't been able to do since my mom gave me that record player for my high school graduation present.

Let me know sometime.

ILY, John

8 p.m., 7-21 "7 Messages?"
Hey, Sweet Frog Prince, that is just what I need. Lots of communication does it for me. After our second conversation this morning I felt much better, much more a part of what is going on in our lives, despite your bad news from Washington. It is just like you to brush it off, like a bothersome mosquito!

I do believe I have a record player which will play old records. 33 rpm Beethoven records should work, so don't throw them away. Keep them with your bike and whatever seems like good things to have.

Tomorrow exercise again and then probably some errands to run. I should be home in the early afternoon, in case you call. So far the weekend looks quiet. God keep you safe in his care tonight and always. I feel your love around me, holding me close which is the way I want it. Goodnight my love, Joan

Late afternoon, 7-22
Hi,
I think your question "Are you happy?" caught me a little off guard. Fair enough of you to ask, as that is what we are both about now, isn't it: being the source of each other's happiness?

It's hard to have "joy" at a time like this, of course, with my professional reputation maybe on the line.

But for me, Joan, "happiness" where you are concerned is now a life-long concept and it transcends anything going on in my difficult "office world" right now. Don't forget that you've been in my "innards" for nearly seven decades, and right now I'm counting on the realization that after all that time "my" prize is within reach, even though six months ago that reach wasn't even in my thinking.

That's why I believe that we are part of God's plan, that, for me, the happiness that has been missing most of my adult life finally is about to become a reality. You've had happiness with Cliff, lots of it, and I may or may not measure up after a year or so, but I know that you're the kind of woman who is going to give me—and yourself—every chance imaginable to feed off each other and love each other passionately and *never* take the other for granted. If I ever forget to open a door for you, for example :-), you should remind me with that awesome smile of yours. All the little things I've learned, some the hard way, I promise to bring to our marriage and make it as good or better for you than your first 50-plus. Now that is a *real* challenge, but that's what "happiness" is for me, to keep my eyes on that challenge through these uncharted shoals, knowing that you're here with me to help *us* put it all together.

So the next time we stroll hand-in-hand on that Kirkland waterfront, we'll be even more "noticeable" than we were on July 4. You'll have *my* ring and I'll have *your* heart and the whole world just might be a little better for it. I just pray that God will give us each enough more years of reasonably good health that we can fulfill each other's potential as active, loving seniors who will continue (as you have been for a long time, already) to make a difference in our community. That's going to be a new deal for me and I'll need some guidance from you, but I expect it to be part of our "love package" and, yes, that is what "happiness" means, among a number of other things.

Well, that was more than I had intended to say, but it seemed to flow from my heart pretty easily.

My love for you has no bounds and I need new words to express it as fully as I'd like to. I cling to your spirit, my Precious One.

Good night.
John

6 p.m. 7-22
"My Heart"
Yes, my Darling, my heart is yours already, and I have already given myself to you. Marriage vows are for the world to see, but

I have already committed myself to you for the rest of my life, and you can take that as an absolute.

You answered my question, "Are you happy?", so perfectly for me that I would give you an A++++++ and more if I were grading it. Everything you said filled me with that sense of total belief that you and I belong together and that our union holds all the joys and satisfaction that anyone can ever hope for. I promise you that it will continue to be my purpose in life to make you happy and keep you happy. WE are going to have a lot of togetherness to make up for all the years we have missed. The deep love and passion that we feel for each other now astounds me. I had no idea that this could happen to people our age. Maybe we are extraordinary, but I hope there are others who can experience the same kind of joy in being together at this stage of life. It is miraculous to me.

I have fun with you, John. I am proud of you and proud to be with you. I like you as well as I love you. I want to be with you and have my friends and family know you, and have you be part of my life in every way, just as I want to be part of your life in every way. WE are good together. Thank God. I can hardly wait until we marry but for me there is no difference in the commitment I feel right now. *I am already yours.*

Beyond that, I will continue to pray for you as I constantly do, and for us as I constantly do. God bless you, keep you always in His care, make you strong and well, and bless our love that we together may serve Him well, now and forever.

You are my love, John. I am so excited to look forward to life with you beside me every day and every night. My love is deep and real and forever. Joan

8 p.m., 7-22
My Most Precious, "Laughter and Love"

Your love letters are so powerful, Joan, I can only read them through misty eyes. I've only now been able to read and re-read yours today, after getting back from my still-functioning office. You are such a marvel to me, after pining for you for most of my life to realize that you are light-years beyond all and anything I could have imagined.

I almost panic when I think of one of us being hurt or getting sick or some other terrible happening before we can marry and I can have my first-ever night with you knowing for sure that there will be countless more, without interruption, where we both can truly relax and watch the sun come up if we want to. Even at the beach, there was a feeling of hurry-you-don't-have-enough-time. That is my big challenge now, to be patient and wait for all of this to play out—as it surely will—and then without wasting a day we'll head for Honolulu!

I've already forgotten what we were laughing about on the phone, or maybe it was just me, but I'm so starved for laughter after all these years. I could spend days just looking at all those pictures of you around your home, that's all you seem to do, is smile and laugh as you enjoy life. How I need that!

ILY
John

7:30 p.m., 7-23
My Darling, for sure one reason we laugh a lot is just because we are so happy to be together. I love the feeling of laughing with you, having fun with our life. It seems to happen whether we are writing e-mails, talking on the phone or being physically together. Take *that* anyway you like. We *are* happy together. And I want more.

I really like it when you phone, so we can talk. Twice today was good. It will be wonderful if you can find your way to Mercer Island tomorrow. I would really like to be able to tell you my impressions of our class "Mini—Reunion" in person. I'll have to get up on *your* schedule in the morning, probably 6:30 A.M. I will be picking Ann up at my church parking lot at 8:00. She thinks she can find the Elks Club. I have no clue, so it is good she will be with me. Next time there is a reunion, you and I will go together. I will like that. By then our notoriety should have calmed down???? We can be brazen and act like lovers, which we will be, and our classmates will wish they are like we are.

Today I have put a lot of hours into outside work. I started by watering all of the potted stuff on my deck and close to the front door. I cut back wilted blossoms and generally tidied up. Then I got into serious clean up of the shade garden off the back side of the deck, under the split leaf maple, the pine and hemlock dripping with long strands of ivy. I cut back ivy, cleaned up the winter's drop of needles, planted some arugula, pruned several things that were out of control, etc. I probably worked from noon to six with some breaks in between. I am not finished by any means, but I finally am making progress. The weather and my heavy activities at the museum this year have kept me from doing this stuff on my regular schedule. Next year you can help. Actually, you have already been a big help this year, which is pretty neat. But believe me, I am not marrying you to get a yard-work guy!

When I first went out to work in my shade garden, I stood on the deck and could see a neighbor's cat, Josh, sitting at the foot of my bird bath. Then he jumped up to the top of the bird bath and sat on the edge. I rushed into the house to get my camera, but he jumped down before I could get the picture. I called him by name and scolded him. He replied by coming over and rubbing against me, then jumping into my lap. So we had a time of cat massage, which he liked a lot.

In the meantime, overhead in the trees above, the vine maple close to the deck, the pine and hemlocks a little farther out, I saw lots of birds. There was one hummingbird, and several very small birds, two different kinds which I didn't know. There are always so many birds in my yard. I thought of you, how you cherish your bird sanctuary, and I decided that you will probably be fulfilled in *our* yard full of birds, as well. You can teach me about them. I have not studied birds like you, but I do love them, too. You can provide feeders if you want. This yard is full of food for them, but you can do whatever you like to attract more and I will love it. I love you for the things that you care about. Birds being one, but there are so many other things that you cherish: Jesus, this country, kindness, family, God's love and His beautiful creation, intelligence, compassion, friends, education, giving back, thankfulness, helping others, and ME. That is a partial list of what I see in you. It is what makes me love you, besides the way you kiss me and make love to me. How lucky can one girl get?!

I hope I get to be with you tomorrow, but I understand that we have to go with the circumstances. There will be a time in the not too distant future when we will be together day and night. The thought fills me with happiness. I love you, John. The wait will be worth it. I promise. Joan

John is able to visit Joan at her home, briefly, after she returns from their class reunion.

5:20, 7-24
"If I give my love to you,
will you give me all your love?
Will you promise to be true to me,
like the stars that shine above?

If I give you all my love,
Will you handle it with care?"

Those are the first words of one of the songs I find myself singing. I don't remember them all, but many, and I keep finding myself humming or singing them.

I have no doubts about the answers. You need have no doubts either.

I am always comforted when we can be together. This afternoon was a lovely, if brief, romantic experience. I wish it had been longer. But then I always wish that. The time will come.

John, You made me very happy this afternoon. My calendar is marked with happy occasions. I keep thinking if someone were to ask me if I'm "dating," how could I answer? Everything that has happened between us has no connection with what anyone would call a typical dating pattern. I don't think we have had a "date." All of our togetherness has proved to be a commitment of one kind or another. All of those commitment occasions have pulled us together in stronger and stronger togetherness. I think it has to be a deep love for one another that makes it be this way.

7-26, p.m.
Today (Tuesday) was busy and long. Tomorrow will be much more so. This morning, I discovered that for some reason, I had a big bruised area around my left eye. Maybe I rubbed it to much, or washed too hard. When I started to put on my eye make up, there was this big black and blue spot. During the day the black and blue started draining down to my upper cheek. Tomorrow, I am going to model an absolutely fabulous expensive black hat which is an art piece for sale at the Patron's Party. I hope I can hide my battered look with make-up. If not someone else may have to wear the hat, but it looks really good on me without the bruise.

11 a.m. 7-27
Hi,

If you have time to read this before you crash late tonight, okay. If not, it can wait til morning.

I'm really concerned about your eye, Precious. That doesn't sound good. Do you bruise easily? Maybe too much aspirin? I presume your doctor knows about this "tendency." Face it, we're both "damaged goods" so we need to pay attention to these things. Seems you've mentioned something similar before.

I suppose I'll never get to see the hat on you, but the idea is very tempting and luscious. Stay with this, you can be a model at 80 and I'll be in the front row making loud applause. Unfortunately (or is it?) 80 isn't that far off so we need to get cracking on missed time. So much to see, so many places to visit. Mind-numbing, isn't it? ILY, John

1915, 7-27
My Sunshine (*Radiant*, that is!),
I've been praying all day that you're not going to over-exert in this hot weather, that your bruise will heal quickly, and that you'll get home safely and with enough energy to at least get the front door open. I'd give a ransom to be that mouse in your pocket today, Jo-an in her element, wowing everyone she meets, hat or no hat. Oh, how I love her and miss her and want to have her and how jealous I'm going to be having to share her with her "public," eventually. That's very presumptuous of me, My Precious, and I can't help it. But that kind of "jealousy" really will be *pride*, for me, because I will have joined the most outstanding woman I've ever known or could even imagine. Think of it this way, Jo-an Elizabeth (love that combination), for me this is like being suddenly assigned to the White House as W's closest advisor, a dream that no one would dare have. And yet there you are, saying you love me as much as I love you and I can't even calculate how to express that depth of commitment.

Well, I've said more than enough for one sitting and am thinking there's got to be something to eat here in my little fridge, not Jo-an quality, but *something.* So, no matter what time it is as you read this, know for sure that my love for you is like the tsunami I watched on TV last night: Nothing can compare to its power.

9:30 p.m., 7-27
My Darling,
That was the perfect message to come home to after a long hard but satisfying day. Guess what? I sold that luscious hat right off my head to a beautiful young blonde woman whose husband was absolutely sure she needed it. They paid $159.00 for it. I had worn it for at least an hour and a half and had had many

compliments. Three people took my picture, two of them who would be selling them on the Internet, so I'll be able to check to see if they are any good and maybe will get one for you. A friend took some too, but by then I had switched to another hat. It was good, but not as great as the first. We'll see.

John, it is so wonderful that each time we are together we discover new things about each other and so far, for me at least, every thing that happens makes me love you more. I was afraid I would not be able to make half way intelligent party conversation, but I was ok in spite of the fact that it all was in the back of my mind throughout the entire evening.

I have never been so happy in my whole life as I am with you John. It is incredible. When I got into my top down convertible (safe at night on Mercer Island) and left my friends' house where I had parked—I rode with them to Bellevue and back—I smiled all the way home thinking about us and how relaxed and good we are together, how much fun we have, how we complement each other and accept each other as we are. No need to change a thing. We fit. It must be a God-given blessing. I keep saying thank you to our Lord for giving us each other. How else could it be so perfect? There is no way to express in words the love I feel for you. I will have to prove it by actions through the days and years that lie ahead. I pray there will be many.

John, you have invaded my life, filled my life, and become the major focus of my life. I cannot even begin to imagine it without you. Everything I can think of is filled with you. It all is an overwhelming situation to me, and I cannot imagine the rest of my years without you.

You have professed your love for me since we were in first grade. I believe that, but you have to know that my love for you, although not nearly for as long a time, makes up for it in volume. Believe it John. I am totally gone on this relationship and absolutely thrilled that you want me. I want you, I love you and I will be with you in whatever situation we can share.

I am here for you always, I love you far beyond any sensible thought or program. It feels like a God-given blessing. I pray that it is.

CHAPTER 12

Joan's Love Story

Fast-forwarding now to September 2005, the critical Inspector's Report was reviewed at a higher level and found to be seriously flawed. John's group, and John too, received an official clean bill of health. Within a week of receiving this welcome news, Joan wrote her own version of the love story she and John shared together. She hoped the world would know, some day, through its publication.

My Love Story 10 p.m., 9-1

In March 2003, shortly after my husband Cliff died, I received a compassionate e-mail message from John. It was kind, touching and supporting and helpful to me to know that my friend from first grade and through most of my school years cared enough to send it.

It was followed by several messages throughout the following year which were obviously meant to help me over the rough times of recent widowhood. John had told me he was concerned about my well being, and it was obvious to me that he wanted to help me as a long time friend. I enjoyed hearing from him, but nothing more ever entered my mind.

I started going occasionally to our Sumner High School Lunch Bunch monthly meetings at the I-Hop in Tacoma, just to have a connection with people who had been a big part of my growing up years. People who know who you were, and know about your family and your history, provide a certain stability that newer friends never can give. I liked feeling a part of my old class again. It was a comfort to me to be accepted and included in this familiar group of people with whom I had shared many years.

John came to those gatherings whenever his work schedule would permit. We seldom sat near each other. Once or twice we talked a while after everyone else had left, just friendly talk, but John always made me feel he was concerned about my well being and wanted me to be happy. I considered it the caring of an old friend.

Through the following months we began to exchange more e-mails. We made lists of questions for each other to answer about our interests, likes and dislikes, political persuasions, religious beliefs, whether or not we liked theatre, symphony, classical music, popular music, dancing, sports, what did we read, how about gardening, travel, on and on. It turned out that we were amazed to discover that we were so much on the same page about most everything. We learned to really appreciate each other and our friendship grew. We began to know each other well. We learned to respect each other as individuals who held the same beliefs and liked the same things. We were good friends.

We shared interests, ideas, opinions, and a desire to spend the rest of our lives in certain ways. We agreed on almost all of these hopes. We began to feel more and more relaxed and comfortable with each other. We had fun exchanging feelings.

Eventually we had a few telephone conversations, finally we decided to meet in my home for coffee and conversation. It was the meeting of two old friends, that was all, except that the seeds of love were planted that day. They were deep in the soil of our souls. It didn't take long before they sprouted and rose up toward the sun and blossomed into a glorious love that has deep, enduring roots. It is sure to last at least as long as we live. I promise to love and to cherish John for the rest of my life. My name is Joan.

EPILOGUE

And so Joan and John were married in Honolulu on November 25, 2005 at the Outrigger Canoe Club, under a palm tree and by a Hawaiian clergyman. They chose Honolulu because Hawaii makes it easy for people to marry, no residency requirements, no blood tests, just $60 for a license and an interview at the license bureau. Of course, Honolulu was Joan's favorite city, away from the Mainland. And with just the two of them involved (no bridesmaid, no best man) they could concentrate entirely on each other, something they had been waiting to do for what seemed an eternity.

They returned to Joan's home as man and wife, and all who knew them marveled at the love they showed for each other, always smiling, gazing into each other's eyes, holding hands, appearing as twenty-something newly-weds. John moved into Joan's lovely home, overlooking Lake Washington, and quickly became part of her wide circle of loving friends. In their home, their married life together was one to be envied. They never had a quarrel, much less a real fight. They loved, and made love to, each other with passion usually reserved for the gods.

John took Joan to one of his favorite steelhead fly-fishing streams, the Grand Ronde River in southeastern Washington state, and she painted a picture of him there, fly rod in hand. Joan took John to Sonoma Country and the wine-tasting weekend. He expanded Joan's bird sanctuary, installed 24-hour lighting for her front yard flag pole, built a drip irrigation system to automatically water her many potted flowers, worked with her in her well-worn kitchen, with never a misstep.

They attended a Hillsdale College Leadership Seminar in Seattle and there were photographed with Carl Rove, one of their favorite political personalities.

They visited Victoria's fabulous natural history museum and Vancouver Island's lovely Buchart Gardens, for Joan, especially, a flower-lover's paradise. In her "top down" silver convertible they drove to Yellowstone Park and on the way they stopped so that Joan could paint the beauty of the snow-capped Gallatin Range. The following year, to the Grand Canyon and Sedona's Red Rock formations, which Joan had never seen before, returning to Mercer Island through Utah's glorious Canyon Country. They did a rental-car trip through the Southeastern United States, a first for both of them: Monticello, the Wright Brothers' Kitty Hawk, historic Charleston and plantation country, returning via the Gettysburg Battlefield National Park.

They traveled abroad together, returning to Honolulu every late-November to celebrate their wedding anniversary and to send Christmas cards to their many friends. While there, John helped Joan learn how to snorkel at Hanauma Bay, she at age 78!

Other travels took them to places neither had seen before: A Yangtze River boat cruise from Shanghai to Beijing, via Xian, home to the fabulous terra cotta soldiers, for Joan, especially, an artist's dream come true. They did a river boat cruise on the Danube River, from the Black Sea upstream into Germany. Holland America Line took them from Santiago to Rio de Janeiro; later through the Mediterranean Sea, including Florence, Pompeii and ancient Carthage. Then the Panama Canal, from Florida to California and in 2010 Alaska and its mighty glaciers. In Fall 2010 they booked a cruise to Northern Europe for June 2011, but Joan's recurring breast cancer and dementia—which had been creeping inexorably since Spring

2010—made that trip impossible. She had joked with John that she would never leave her beloved home—she had designed and built it in 1966—that "They'll have to carry me out of here feet first."

And that is what happened. Joan died in bed alongside an already-grieving John, early in the morning of June 23, 2011.

Five years of completely loving bliss, just as they had promised each other on that Tiffany Monday.

Finis

Paints on the Grand Ronde River

Painting Fly Fisherman John

The Finished Product

With Carl Rove

John with Kites

Exercise Class Leader

Painting the Gallatin Range

Joan and Top-Down Convertible

Joan in Red Rock Country

Formal Night, South American Cruise

Joan with Best Buddy Geneve at 55th High School Reunion, Summer 2002

Honolulu Wedding

AFTERWORD

Most proceeds from the sale of this book will be donated to the Alzheimer's Association and the Fred Hutchison Cancer Research Center (in collaboration with the Seattle Cancer Care Alliance), worthy organizations whose purpose is to learn more about, and eventually how to defeat, the scourges that took Joan's life.

ABOUT THE AUTHOR

John Sager is a retired United States intelligence officer whose services for the Central Intelligence Agency, in various capacities, spanned more than a half-century. He now lives in the Covenant Shores retirement community on Mercer Island, Washington. There, the walls of his new bachelor pad—he calls it Joan's Gallery—are adorned with her exquisite water color paintings, acrylics and batiks, ever-lasting reminders of his radiant Sunshine.